Contemporary

Foundations

Writing

The McGraw·Hill Companies

Photo Credits

Photo on page 21, © Image Source/Getty Images
Photo on page 40, © Robynrg/Shutterstock Images, LLC
Photo on page 87, © Getty Images
Photo on page 95 (l), © Getty Images
Photo on page 95 (r), © Corbis

www.WrightGroup.com

Printed in the United States of America

Send all inquiries to:
Wright Group/McGraw-Hill
P. O. Box 812960
Chicago, IL 60681

ISBN: 978-1-4045-7634-6
MHID: 1-4045-7634-7

1 2 3 4 5 6 7 8 9 10 COU 12 11 10 09 08

The McGraw-Hill Companies

Contents

Contents

Introduction

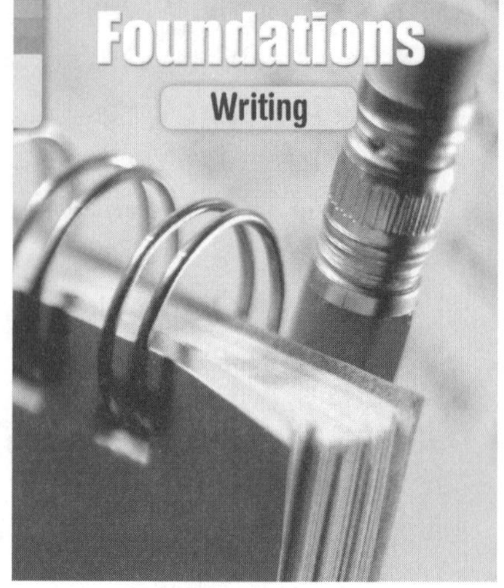

Welcome to Contemporary's *Foundations: Writing*. This book will help you improve your writing. It will also help you improve your reading and thinking skills.

Part I: Writing helps you practice the four stages of the writing process.

Prewriting—planning and organizing
Drafting—writing by following your plan
Revising—evaluating and rewriting
Editing—correcting grammar, mechanics, and usage problems

You will learn about five kinds of essays and practice writing these essays.

Descriptive Essay
Personal Narrative
How-To Essay
Essay of Example
Comparison-and-Contrast Essay

Part II: Grammar is a language-skills workbook. It explains important language skills that writers need to understand.

Grammar—nouns, pronouns, verbs, adjectives, and adverbs
Punctuation—periods, question marks, exclamation marks, commas, and semicolons
Sentence Structure—incomplete sentences, run-on sentences, and comma splices

These special features in *Foundations: Writing* will help you practice your writing skills.

In Your Journal—ideas to think about and write about on your own
Language Tip—explanations, pronunciations, study hints, and background information that will help you understand what you are reading
Test Skills—a reminder that this skill is often tested on standardized tests
With a Partner—reading, writing, and thinking activities to do with a classmate, family member, or friend
Posttest—a test, evaluation chart, and answer key so you will know how well you have mastered the skills

We hope you will enjoy *Foundations: Writing*. We wish you the best of luck with your studies!

Foundations

Contemporary's *Foundations* is a series of books designed to help you improve your skills. Each book provides skill instruction, offers interesting passages to study, and gives opportunities to practice what you are learning. In addition to *Foundations: Writing,* we invite you to explore these books.

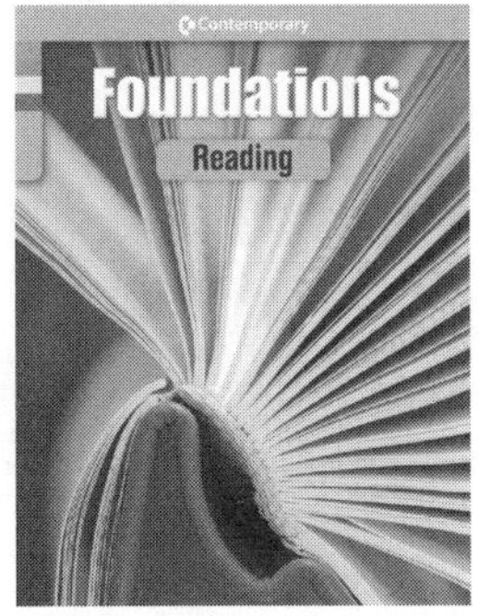

- In *Foundations: Reading,* you will read **practical information, nonfiction, poetry,** and **short stories.**
- You will learn to find the **main point** and the **details;** identify **fact, opinion,** and **bias;** make **inferences;** read **photographs** and **cartoons;** and understand **rhythm, rhyme, plot,** and **theme.**
- **Writing Workshops, Language Tips,** and **prereading questions** will help you become a better reader, writer, and thinker.

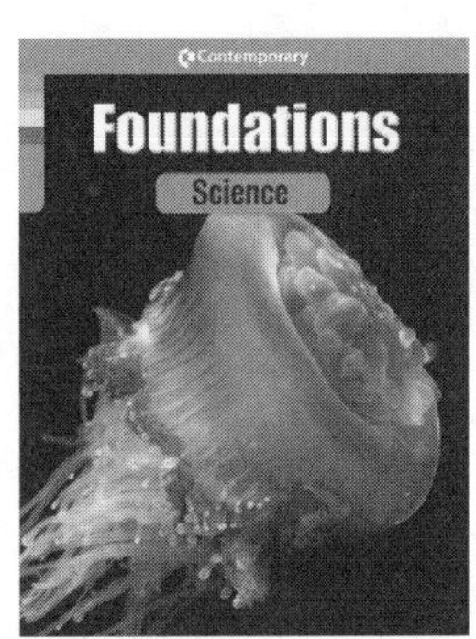

- In *Foundations: Science,* you will learn about the **human body, plant biology, physics, chemistry,** and **Earth science.**
- You will practice putting events in **order; reading diagrams, charts,** and **graphs;** using the **scientific method;** and making **comparisons and contrasts.**
- **Try It Yourself!** activities will guide you through simple experiments so you will have a better understanding of what you have been reading about. **Writing Workshops** and **Language Tips** will help you use your reading and writing skills to think about science topics.

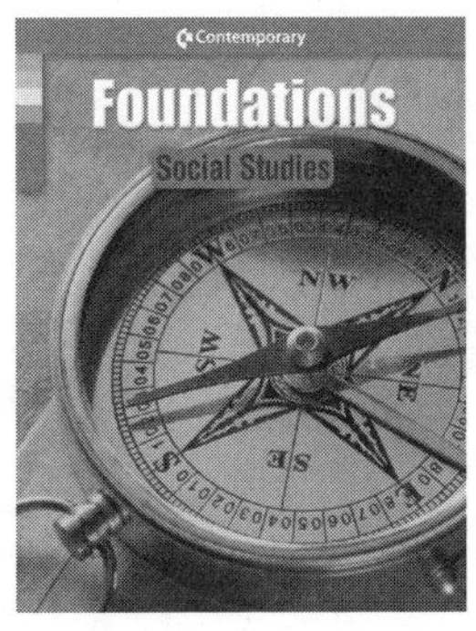

- In *Foundations: Social Studies,* you will learn about **world history, U.S. history, civics and government, geography,** and **economics.**
- You will **summarize,** make **predictions,** infer the main idea of **cartoons,** find information on **maps,** and read various kinds of **graphs.**
- **Background Information, Language Tips,** and **Writing Workshops** will let you use what you already know as you read and write about social studies topics.

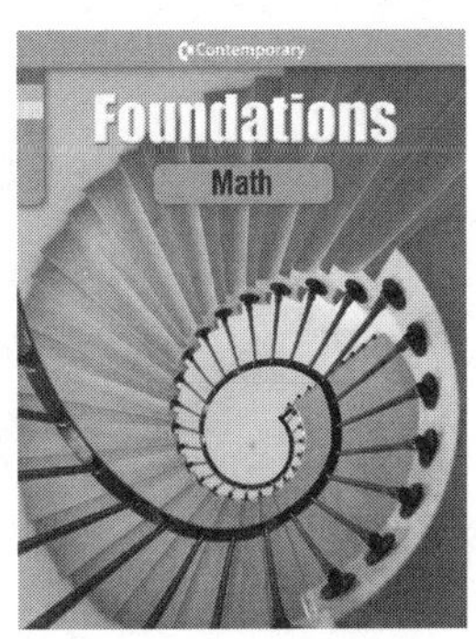

- In *Foundations: Math,* you will practice using **whole numbers, money, decimals, fractions, ratios,** and **percents.**
- Exercises will help you review the **addition, subtraction, multiplication,** and **division** facts; **round numbers; estimate** answers; and solve **word problems.**
- **Math Notes, On Your Calculator,** and **Language Tips** will help you improve your math skills.

PART I

Writing

Dear Amalia,

I suppose you've heard the news. Last Monday, after three days and nights of rain, it finally happened. The river behind our home flooded.

On the morning of the 15th, the people in the neighborhood started sandbagging the river. We worked all day and into the night. But on the evening of the 16th, the river broke through. Water poured into our yards, our homes, and our cars.

The flood did a lot of damage. We are all still cleaning up. But the way everyone has pulled together has helped. For the first time since we moved here, we feel like part of the community. People here are a lot more willing to help each other than I thought.

Sincerely,

Russ

Chapter 1

Test Skill

The Essay

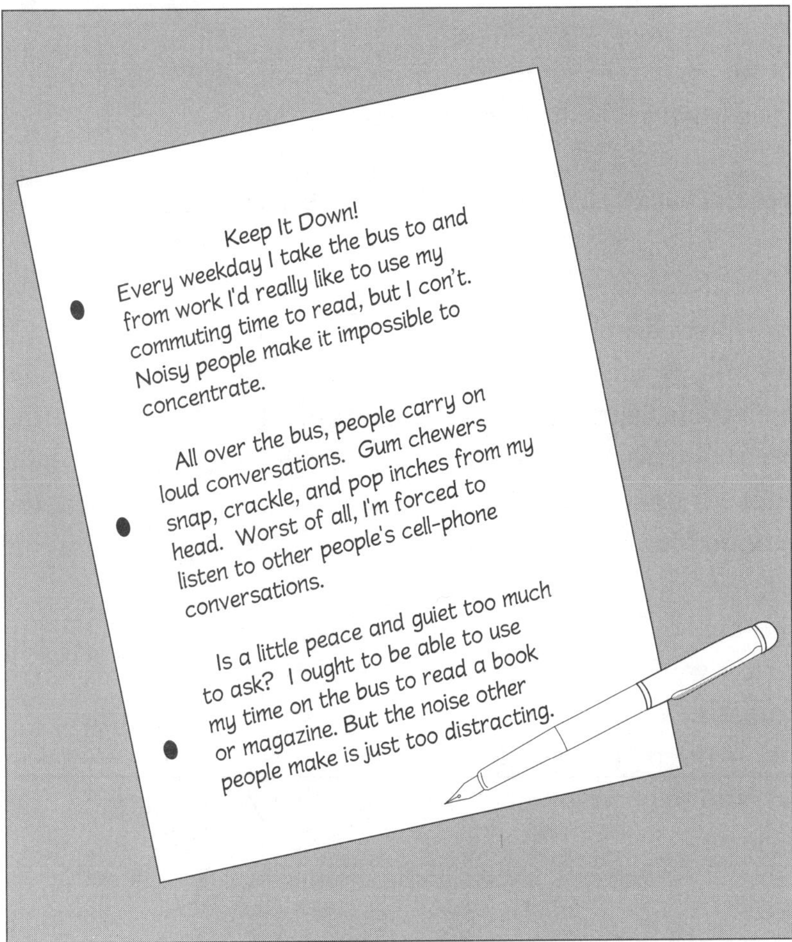
Keep It Down!

Every weekday I take the bus to and from work I'd really like to use my commuting time to read, but I can't. Noisy people make it impossible to concentrate.

All over the bus, people carry on loud conversations. Gum chewers snap, crackle, and pop inches from my head. Worst of all, I'm forced to listen to other people's cell-phone conversations.

Is a little peace and quiet too much to ask? I ought to be able to use my time on the bus to read a book or magazine. But the noise other people make is just too distracting.

Read the short essay pictured above. It describes a bus rider's complaint. Why does a writing book begin by having you read? Reading and writing go hand in hand. Good reading skills help you write well. And good writing skills help you become a better reader. This book will teach you how to read essays while you learn how to write essays. In this chapter, you'll take a closer look at the essay form.

After working through this chapter, you should be able to

- name the three parts of an essay
- describe the purpose of each part
- find the main idea of an essay

The Parts of an Essay

A good essay has a clear beginning, middle, and end. Writers call these parts the introduction, the body, and the conclusion. All three parts of an essay have one thing in common. All three are about the same main idea.

The Introduction

The **introduction** of an essay tells you what the essay is about. Reread the first paragraph of the essay shown at the beginning of this chapter.

> Every weekday I take the bus to and from work. I would really like to use my commuting time to read, but I can't. Noisy people make it impossible to concentrate.

Can you see how this first paragraph introduces you to the rest of the essay? The first sentence tells you the **topic**, or subject of the essay. In this case, the topic is *bus rides*. The second sentence tells you a little more about the topic. It lets you know that the writer has a complaint about riding on the bus. Then, in the last sentence, the writer says, "Noisy people make it impossible to concentrate." This sentence states the main idea of the essay. The **main idea** lets you know more specifically what the writer will say about the topic.

As you can see, the main idea narrows down the topic. It limits the subject to one or two points that the writer wants to make. The writer of the bus essay has narrowed the topic to one main point—the other riders on the bus make too much noise.

Notice that the essay is titled "Keep It Down!" The title is a clue about the main idea. Titles are usually brief, and they are often clever. The writer hopes that the title will catch the reader's attention.

A good introductory paragraph does two important things:

- introduces the topic
- states the main idea

Exercise 1

PART A

Read the essay. Then underline the main idea in the introduction.

Who Is Hiring?

Getting a job begins with finding a job opening. You can find job openings in a number of ways.

Check the want ads in your local newspaper. Don't be afraid to ask friends and relatives if they know of any jobs. Call companies that you think you would like to work for. Register with both private and government job agencies.

These suggestions will help you find out who is hiring. They are the first step toward finding a job.

PART B

Read the middle and the end of this essay. Then circle the letter of the paragraph that would make a good introduction.

ABCs of Interviewing

Above all, be on time. You do not have to wear expensive clothes, but dress neatly. Act confidently. Look the interviewer in the eye, and answer questions completely and honestly. Show that you know you can do the job.

A successful interview can bring you the job you want. If you follow these guidelines, you will find yourself that job!

(a) While an interview can make you very nervous, it gives you a chance to make a good first impression. Make the most of your chance. Be sure you know what to do at a job interview.

(b) Job interviews can be hard. Answering questions is not easy. Sometimes you even have to go back for a second interview. Try to stay calm.

Check your answers on page 182.

The Body

The **body** of an essay tells more about the main idea. Reread the middle paragraph of the essay about riding the bus. As you read, think about the main idea of the essay: Noisy people make it impossible to concentrate.

All over the bus, people carry on loud conversations. Gum chewers snap, crackle, and pop inches from my head. Worst of all, I'm forced to listen to other people's cell-phone conversations.

Can you see how the body explains the main idea? Each sentence gives examples of noisy riders. The ideas in the body of an essay are called **supporting details**. That is because they help support, or explain, the main idea. This diagram shows how the main idea and the supporting details relate to each other.

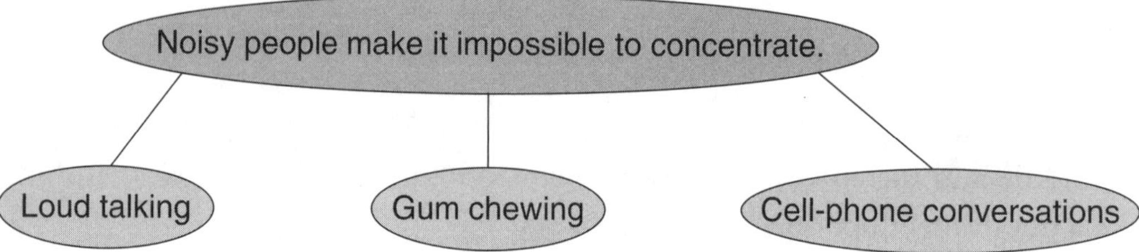

Each detail in the body tells a little more about the main idea. Each detail helps the reader understand what the writer means.

The body of an essay does one important thing:

- supports the main idea

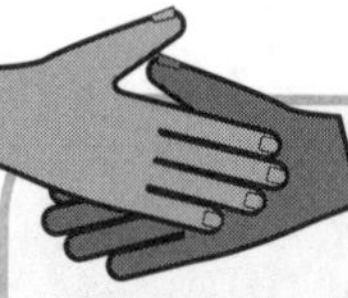

With a Partner

Tell your partner to imagine writing an essay. Then ask your partner one of these main-idea questions. Explain that each answer could be a detail in the body of an essay.

- What are five things you'd do if you won a million dollars?
- What are five things you'd hate to live without?
- What are five things you'd like to be remembered for?

When your partner is finished, have him or her ask you one of the questions.

Exercise 2

PART A

Read the essay. The main idea has been underlined. Then list the three supporting details.

My Dream House

My dream home would be a nice bungalow. There are many features that I would like this home to have. <u>Three features stand out as most important.</u>

First, I want the home to have two bedrooms. Then my son, Louis, could have his own room, and he would not have to sleep on the couch. I also want the house to have a big basement. The basement would be a good place for my husband, Big Lou, to set up a workshop. Finally, I'd like the living room to have a fireplace. I've always loved how fireplaces make rooms feel cozy.

I may never get such a home. But I can dream, can't I?

What three features would the woman like her house to have? List these features as the supporting details.

(a) ____________________

(b) ____________________

(c) ____________________

LANGUAGE Tip

Spelling

Words such as *I'd, wouldn't,* and *I've* are **contractions**. The apostrophe replaces letters that have been omitted.

I would = I'd

would not = wouldn't

I have = I've

PART B

Read this introduction to an essay. The main idea has been underlined. Then circle the letter of the body that develops the main idea.

Everybody has a different idea about what the ideal home should be. My dream home would be a great apartment in a high-rise downtown. <u>I'd like to live there for many reasons</u>.

(a) I'm a single guy from a small town. I moved to this city because I got a job here. I work downtown. There are many high-rise apartments buildings downtown.

(b) If I lived in a downtown high-rise, I would be where all the action is. I would also have a great view of the lake, which is only a few blocks from downtown. I would not have to commute to work. I would live near enough to walk.

Check your answers on page 182.

The Conclusion

The **conclusion** sums up the main idea of the essay. Reread the last paragraph of the essay about riding the bus. Can you see how this final paragraph restates the writer's message?

> Is a little peace and quiet too much to ask? I ought to be able to use my time on the bus to read a book or magazine. But the noise other people make is just too distracting.

The first two sentences emphasize the point that the writer wants to make. The last sentence restates the main idea: "Noisy people make it impossible to concentrate."

Notice that the conclusion doesn't bring up new ideas. For example, it doesn't tell about other bus problems, such as late buses or high fares. Instead, the conclusion "wraps up" the main idea that has already been explained.

A concluding paragraph does one important thing:

- restates the main idea of the essay

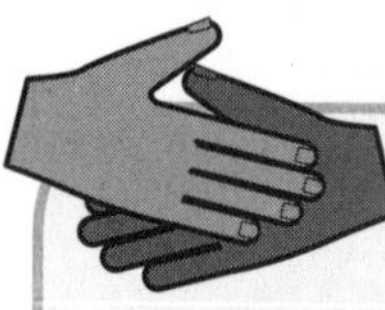

With a Partner

Think of a famous person you admire. List five or six important details that describe the person. Then read your list to a partner. Ask your partner to make up one or two sentences that could be the conclusion to your essay.

Exercise 3

PART A

Read the essay. The main idea has been underlined. Then underline the sentence in the conclusion that restates the main idea.

The Day My World Fell Apart

Three years ago, my wife asked me for a divorce. The day she confronted me was the worst day of my life.

At first, I could not believe it. I felt sick to my stomach. Then I demanded to know why. She told me, and I tried to understand. However, I still felt sick.

My world seemed to turn upside down the day LaTise asked for a divorce. Three years later, I am still trying to cope with the loss.

PART B

Read the introduction and the body to this essay. The main idea has been underlined. Then read the two choices for the conclusion. Circle the letter of the conclusion that restates the main idea.

A Necessary Evil

The hardest thing I ever did was tell my husband I wanted a divorce. I hated to do it. However, the divorce was really necessary.

We had not loved each other for a long time. We argued far too often. He got on my nerves, and I got on his. We were just living together. We were not really a husband and wife loving each other and working together.

(a) Divorce is never easy. My divorce was especially tough. My brother and his wife also got divorced last year. They should have tried harder to work out their problems.

(b) A divorce was really best for both of us. I am now a happy single woman instead of a miserable Mrs. My ex-husband is happier being unmarried too.

Check your answers on page 182.

The Longer Essay

You have been analyzing very short essays. The essay below follows the pattern you have been studying. It was written by a worker who wanted to convince his company to make a change. As you read the essay, think about the three main parts.

Sample Three-Paragraph Essay

Introduction

It Is About Time

The Waller Company should use flextime to schedule working hours. With flextime, workers would have some say over what time their workday starts and ends. Flextime would benefit both the company and the workers.

Main Idea

Body

For example, flextime could help workers who have children. It would also be good for workers who are "early birds." And the company would benefit because the traffic problem in the parking lot would be solved.

Supporting Details

Conclusion

Clearly the Waller Company should switch to flextime. This method of scheduling would benefit us all.

Restatement of Main Idea

In many ways, the essay is good. It has an introductory paragraph with a clear main idea. The main idea is restated in the conclusion. The body is made up of details that support the main idea.

Notice, however, that the supporting details are not fully explained. For example, the writer says that flextime could help workers who have children. It is not clear why flextime might help. You may be able to guess why, but you should not have to guess. The writer should make the detail clear for you. In other words, the writer should develop the body with details that are more specific.

Sample Longer Essay

Here is a longer, more fully developed version of the three-paragraph essay you just read. The longer essay has the same introduction and conclusion as the other essay. But the body has been expanded. Now each supporting detail is explained in its own paragraph. Each supporting detail has specific details of its own.

Introduction

It Is About Time

The Waller Company should use flextime to schedule working hours. With flextime, workers would have some say over what time their workday starts and ends. Flextime would benefit both the company and the workers.

Body

For example, flextime could help workers who have children. Many working parents have trouble getting their children to daycare early in the morning. This is especially true for parents who travel by bus or train. Workers who have this problem could choose to start later than 8:00 a.m. They could start at 9:30 a.m. and work until 5:30 p.m.

Supporting Detail

Flextime would also be good for workers who are "early birds." These early risers are more productive in the morning. Therefore, they'd be better off starting the work day quite early. For example, some workers might start at 6:30 a.m. and finish at 2:30 p.m.

Supporting Detail

The company, too, would benefit from flex time. That is because the traffic problem in the parking lot would be solved. Right now, everyone is trying to enter or leave the parking lot at the same time. With flextime, that would no longer be the case.

Conclusion

Clearly the Waller Company should switch to flextime. This method of scheduling would benefit us all.

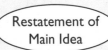

Restatement of Main Idea

The essay is now much easier to understand. It is also more convincing. By adding more details, the writer has built a stronger case for flextime.

Sometimes a main idea can be fully explained in just three paragraphs. But in many cases, writers need more than three paragraphs to make their point.

Exercise 4

PART A

Read the essay. Underline the main-idea sentence in the introduction. Underline the main supporting detail in each paragraph of the body. Then underline the sentence that restates the main idea in the conclusion.

The Good Boss

Over the years, I have worked with many bosses. As a result of working with different kinds of bosses, I have learned what it takes to be a good boss.

First of all, a good boss is fair. A good boss treats everyone equally. No employee is given better treatment than the others or allowed to goof off.

A good boss does not overload employees with work. Sometimes people have to work overtime. Or they may have to work extra hard to meet a deadline. But a good boss makes sure the amount of work is reasonable.

Finally, a good boss knows how to motivate people. A good boss is quick to compliment people on good work. At the same time, a good boss will criticize sloppy work. If someone's work is not done right, a good boss will talk to that person in private. A good boss will try to get the best out of everyone.

In short, a good boss is fair, reasonable, and motivating. It is not easy to have all these qualities. If your boss has them, you are a lucky employee.

PART B

Complete the essay by following the directions in each part.

Introduction

Most people would change some things about themselves if they could. Some people wish they were more patient. Others wish that they were taller or thinner. Here are the three things I would most like to change about myself.

Write your own supporting details on the lines below.

First, ______________________________

Second, ______________________________

Third, ______________________________

First Paragraph of Body

Write a paragraph explaining your first supporting detail.

Second Paragraph of Body

Write a paragraph explaining your second supporting detail.

Third Paragraph of Body

Write a paragraph explaining your third supporting detail.

Conclusion

Write a paragraph that sums up the content of the body and restates the main idea.

Check your answers on page 182.

In Your Journal

From time to time, you will be asked to write in a journal. A journal is a notebook of private writing. In it, you jot down your thoughts about subjects that are interesting to you. Your journal is a place where you can practice writing. Your journal can also serve as a book of writing ideas. When you have an assignment but can't think of anything to write about, look through your journal. See what topics you've already written about.

Here are guidelines for creating a journal of your own.

- **If you can, write in a three-ring or spiral-bound notebook.**
  You are less likely to lose pages if you write in a notebook.
- **Make journal writing a habit.**
  Write in your journal every day (or as often as you can). The more you write, the more comfortable you will become about writing.
- **Write about subjects that are important to you.**
  Describe your wildest hopes and your deepest fears. Write down what you would like to say to your boss, your teacher, or your family. Any subject that is on your mind is a good choice for journal writing.
- **Do not worry about length.**
  Make each entry as long or as short as you like. Begin writing when you have an idea. Stop when you have run out of things to say.
- **Do not worry about making mistakes.**
  Your journal is for your eyes only (unless you choose to show it to someone else). As a result, you do not need to worry about errors when you write in it. Feel free to experiment with different forms of writing. For example, try writing short stories, letters, and poems. Do not be afraid to try out new ideas.
- **Use your journal as a storehouse of ideas.**
  Staple in items that you might like to write about. Store newspaper stories, pictures, cartoons, quotations, song lyrics, and other items of interest.
- **Begin keeping a journal today.**
  Use this topic (or a topic of your own) to get started:
  If you could trade places with somebody for a day, who would it be? Why?

The Writing Process

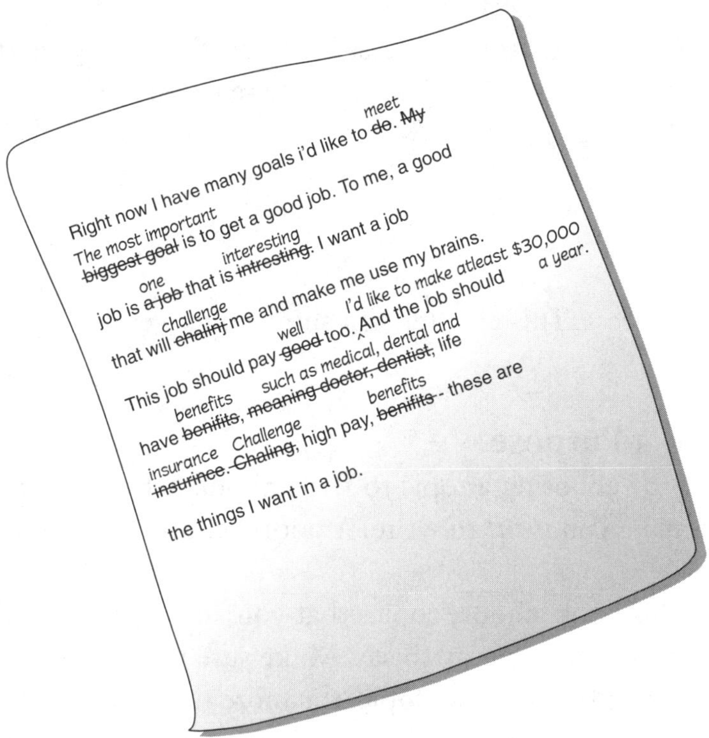

Writing is a process. Writers do not complete good essays in one step. Instead, they go through several stages to get their ideas on paper clearly and logically. Like the student who wrote the paragraph above, writers may make changes along the way. This chapter is a step-by-step guide to planning, writing, and rewriting essays.

After working through this chapter, you will practice each of the four major stages in the writing process:

- prewriting
- drafting
- revising
- editing

Prewriting

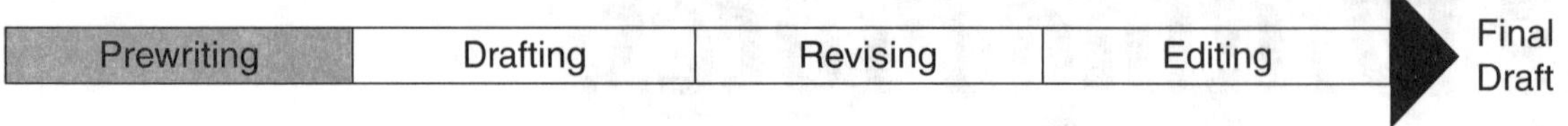

Planning is the first stage in the writing process. This stage is called **prewriting** because you do it *before* you actually write. To plan an essay, take these steps:

- Select a topic and a purpose
- Develop the topic
- Organize your ideas

Prewriting is a flexible process. This chapter will show you several ways of doing each of the steps listed above.

Selecting a Topic and a Purpose

Begin planning an essay by choosing a topic to write about. Select your topic carefully. A well-chosen topic can make you *want* to write. A poorly chosen topic can make writing seem hard and boring.

For the assignments in this book, choose topics that you already know a lot about. You will find it easier to write when you have plenty to say. Make sure the topics you decide to write about interest you. The more interesting the topic, the more fun it is to write.

In addition to a topic, you need a purpose, or reason, for writing. Do you want to explain something? Describe someone or something? Tell the story of an experience you have had? Explaining, describing, and telling a story are the three main purposes you will work with in this book. Let your background, your experiences, and your interests help you decide on a purpose for writing.

For example, suppose you like baseball. If you are good at playing the sport, you might share your know-how. You might explain how to pitch or bunt.

What if you do not play baseball but you love to watch the game? You might describe a game you went to. You can tell your readers what it feels like to sit in the stands and watch your favorite player hit a homerun.

Have you ever watched a game that was decided in the last few seconds of play? You might tell the story of the exciting win.

As you can see, your purpose for writing affects what you write. When you know *why* you are writing, you will have a clearer picture of what you need to say.

Exercise 1

PART A

Put a check mark next to topics that you would like to write about.

- ☐ music
- ☐ TV
- ☐ movies
- ☐ dancing
- ☐ cooking
- ☐ cars
- ☐ sports
- ☐ fashion
- ☐ politics
- ☐ religion
- ☐ family
- ☐ children
- ☐ dating
- ☐ work
- ☐ travel
- ☐ hobbies
- ☐ nature
- ☐ education
- ☐ money
- ☐ friendship

PART B

Select *one* topic that you checked. Decide on a purpose (to explain, to describe, or to tell a story). On a sheet of paper, tell what you plan to say. Follow this example.

Topic: Car

Purpose: To describe

What I plan to say: I am going to write about what it is like to drive my new compact car. I will describe the car inside and out. I will write about how fast the car can go, how smooth the ride is, and how it feels to drive with the top down.

Check your answers on page 182.

In Your Journal

Often good ideas come from everyday events. When something captures your interest, write your ideas in your journal. Later, when you need a topic, look over your notes. You may find an idea that can be expanded into a good essay.

Start creating a pool of ideas now. Choose one of the following "everyday" topics. Then write about it in your journal.

- an interesting item you heard on a TV or radio show
- a funny (or sad) item you read in the newspaper
- something beautiful that you saw on a walk or drive
- an interesting talk you had with a friend

Exercise 2

Developing the Topic

You have decided on a topic and a purpose for writing. What should you do next? Think of supporting details to develop the topic. Sometimes ideas come quickly and easily. At other times, you may need help developing your thoughts. When you have trouble thinking of details that could help you explain your topic, try brainstorming, questioning, or freewriting.

Brainstorming

When you **brainstorm,** you quickly list all your ideas about a subject. Your goal is to come up with as many ideas as you can. Do not take time to judge whether each detail is good or bad. Do not worry about spelling or grammar. Just set a time limit and write down every idea that comes to mind.

Here is a brainstorm list that a student created about the topic of home security. Her purpose was to explain how people can burglarproof their homes before leaving for vacation.

Topic and Purpose: *Explain how to make your home secure*

1. *Lock all doors and windows.*
2. *Stop mail delivery or have trusted neighbor pick up the mail.*
3. *Put lights on timer so they go on and off at usual times.*
4. *Ask trusted friend or neighbor to keep an eye on the house.*
5. *If you have a voice-mail system, check your messages so the system does not fill up.*

Brainstorm about the topic and purpose you chose on page 17.

Topic and Purpose: ____________________

____

____

____

____

____

Check your answers on page 182.

Exercise 3

Questioning

Another way to develop details is **questioning.** When reporters research a story, they ask questions that begin with *Who? What? Where? When? Why?* and *How?* When reporters write their story, the answers to these questions are the details that explain the story. You can use these questions to list the details you need to explain a topic.

Here is how a student answered these questions for his topic and purpose.

Topic and Purpose: To describe my idea of the ideal day.

Who? my girlfriend and I

What? go to the Super Bowl

Where? at the stadium

When? Super Bowl Sunday

Why? to see the game

How? fly to the city where the game is being held

Answering *Who? What? Where? When? Why?* and *How?* can help you brainstorm. If you run out of ideas, use your answers to add more ideas to your list.

How would you spend your ideal day?

Who? ______________________________

What? ______________________________

Where? ______________________________

When? ______________________________

Why? ______________________________

How? ______________________________

Check your answers on page 182.

Freewriting

You have now tried two ways to develop a topic—brainstorming and questioning. A third way to think of ideas is **freewriting**.

To freewrite, set a short time limit. Then write *nonstop* about your topic. Do not lift your pen from the page. If you run out of things to say, write the same word over and over until a thought comes to mind. It is OK if your thoughts wander from topic to topic. Just keep your pen moving and your ideas flowing.

Here is an example of freewriting about a specific topic and purpose.

Topic and Purpose: To describe my idea of the ideal day

Take it nice and slow. Sleep really late. Maybe have breakfast in bed. Have a servant bring me breakfast. Eat, eat, eat, eat, maybe music. Put on my favorite CDs and blast away the neighbors. Better yet, go see my favorite groups in person. Fly to New York. Have a limo pick me up and drive me to the concert.

Freewriting showed the student that she had plenty to say about her topic. If she had had little to say, she might have changed to a different topic or to a different purpose.

Freewriting is also a good way to find a topic and purpose. If you cannot think of a subject, try freewriting about an interesting picture in a magazine. Or freewrite about a person, place, or problem that is on your mind. Then look over what you wrote to see what topics you can find.

The following freewriting was done by a student who needed a topic and a purpose for writing. When she started, she could not think of anything to say. Notice that she just repeated her name until a thought came to mind.

Naidaj Naidaj Naidaj Naidaj. I used to hate my name. Nobody spelled it right. Kids made fun of it. It is funny how kids will pick on anything that is different. Kids want to be just like each other and to belong. Now I love my name. I am named after my grandmother. Like her, I am good at music.

Notice how one thought led to another. Finally the student ended up with several topics to write about.

- how she used to feel about her name and how she feels now
- children need to feel that they belong
- her grandmother's talents that were passed on to her

Exercise 4

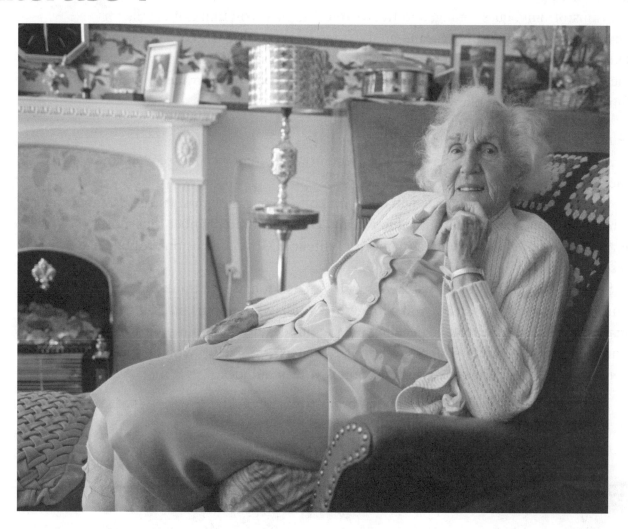

On a piece of paper, freewrite for five minutes about this picture. If you have trouble getting started, combine questioning with freewriting. Use your imagination to write answers to these questions: *Who? What? Where? When? Why? How?*

Check your answers on page 182.

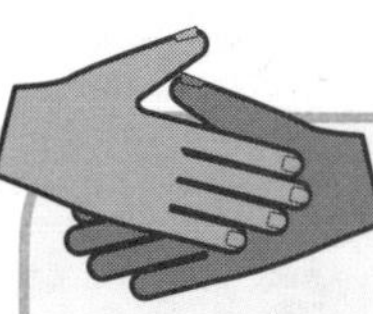

With a Partner

Imagine that you are a reporter. Make a list of interview questions you would like to ask a classmate or friend. Begin each question with *Who? What? Where? When? Why?* or *How?* Interview your partner. Then write the interview in a question-and-answer format.

Organizing Your Ideas

Brainstorming, questioning, and freewriting will help you think of details for developing a topic. The next—and final—stage in prewriting is to **organize** your ideas. During this stage, you begin to shape your ideas into essay form. First, write your main-idea sentence. Then plan the body of your essay by grouping your ideas. When you are finished, your writing plan is complete.

Writing a Main-Idea Sentence

An essay usually contains a main-idea sentence. This sentence lets readers know what the essay is about.

Writing a main-idea sentence will help you collect your thoughts. It will also give you a head start on writing your introduction and conclusion. Remember that most introductions are built around a main-idea sentence. Most conclusions contain a restatement of the main idea.

Sometimes your main idea will be clear to you as soon as you think of a topic and purpose. At other times, it may take longer to decide what important point you want to make. When you have trouble deciding on a main idea, think about your topic and purpose. Look over your supporting details. Then ask yourself, "What are most of the details about?" The answer to this question is your main idea.

To find the main idea of the following brainstorm list, ask yourself, "What are most of the details about?"

Topic and purpose: To explain how to lose weight

- Losing weight helps your heart.
- Do not eat a lot of sugar.
- Set a weekly weight-loss goal.
- Talk yourself out of overeating.
- Stay away from fatty foods.
- Drink plenty of water.
- Picture yourself as thin.
- It is hard but worth it.

What are most of the details about? Most of them are about ways to lose weight. This might be a good main-idea sentence: *Here are some ways to lose those extra pounds.*

Exercise 5

PART A

Write a main-idea sentence for each list of details.

1. Topic and purpose: To explain how to quit smoking

- Stay away from smokers.
- Chew gum.
- Eat in no-smoking areas.
- Suck on sugarless candy.
- Go for walks.
- Do breathing exercises.

Main-idea sentence: ______________________________

____

2. Topic and purpose: To describe my kitchen after the kids cook

- Grease spattered on wall, stove, and floor
- Food stuck to pans
- Strong smell of garlic and burned food
- Dishes floating in sinkful of greasy water

Main-idea sentence: ______________________________

____

3. Topic and purpose: To tell the story of my graduation day

- I woke up with a sore throat and fever.
- We had tornado warnings, and it poured all day.
- The dry cleaners accidentally gave my suit to someone else.
- The car got a flat tire, so I was late for the ceremony.
- I tripped and fell as I started to walk across the stage.

Main-idea sentence: ______________________________

____

PART B

Look over the brainstorming, questioning, and freewriting that you did in this chapter. Choose one list of details. Then write a main-idea sentence to fits your details.

Main-idea sentence: ______________________________

____

Check your answers on page 182.

Grouping Ideas

Writing a main-idea sentence will help you plan the introduction and conclusion of your essay. **Grouping ideas** will help you plan the body of your essay. It helps you decide whether the essay should have one, two, three, or more paragraphs.

To group ideas into paragraphs, look carefully at your list of supporting details. Sometimes all your details are closely related to one another. The ideas form one group. You will be able to write about these ideas in one paragraph. But at other times, your details may belong in two or more groups. Then you will need more than one paragraph for the body.

One way to group ideas is to draw a circle around the details that go together.

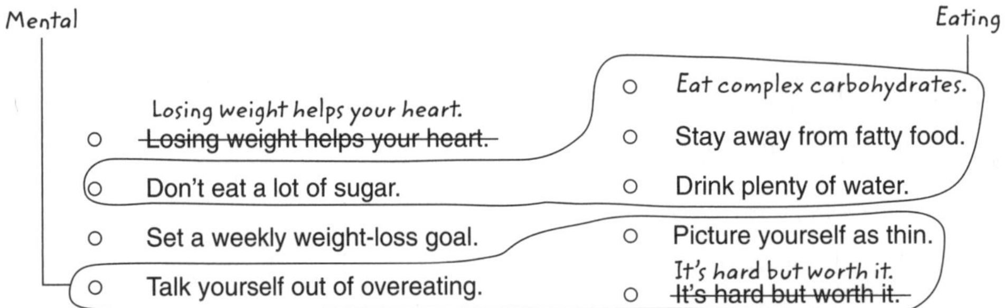

Notice that the writer put the details into two groups. She labeled one group "eating," because all the details are about good eating habits. She labeled the other group "mental," because all the details are about good mental habits. Some of the details did not fit into either group, so the writer crossed them out. Then, as she was grouping ideas, the writer thought of one more supporting detail—eat food high in complex carbohydrates. She added this idea to her list.

Some writers prefer drawing clusters so they can picture how the main idea and details relate to each other. Here is a cluster diagram showing the same details. The center circle contains the main idea. Attached to the main idea are the two clusters, or groups of details.

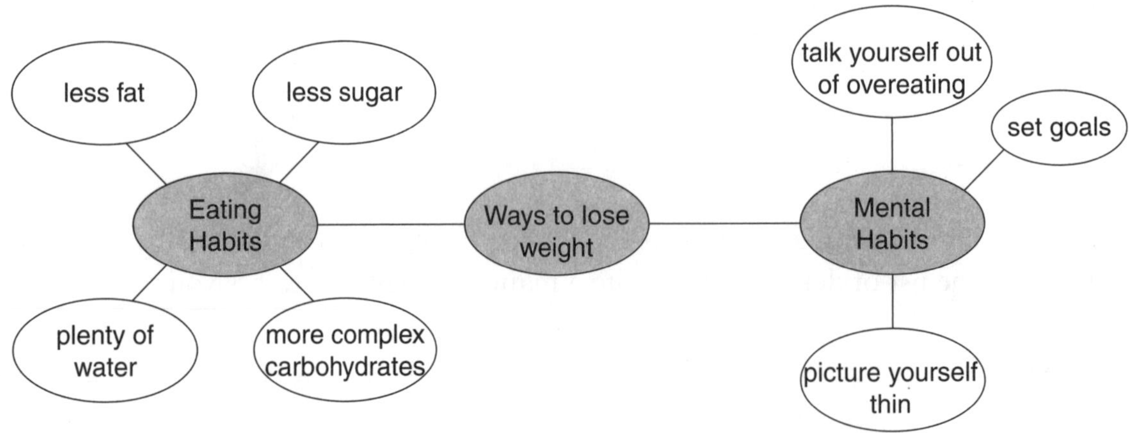

Exercise 6

PART A

Finish putting the ideas in the lists into groups or clusters.

1. Main-idea sentence: I have mixed feelings about getting my own apartment.

- ~~could come and go as I please~~
- ~~will cost a lot~~
- would feel good to be on my own
- would have my own bedroom
- might be kind of lonely
- could play music whenever I want
- hate to cook and clean
- might be kind of lonely
- could play music whenever I want
- hate to cook and clean

Group A: Good Points

(a) could come and go as I please

(b) ____________________

(c) ____________________

(d) ____________________

Group B: Bad Points

(a) will cost a lot

(b) ____________________

(c) ____________________

2. Main-idea sentence: I get many benefits from exercising.

- ~~helps me cope with stress~~
- ~~keeps my weight under control~~
- look better and feel more confident
- proud of sticking to my exercise plan
- have fewer aches and pains
- have more energy

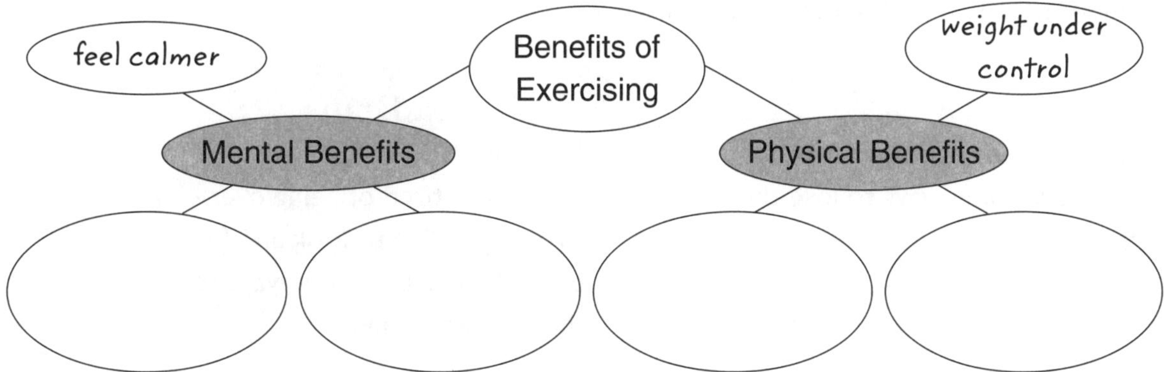

PART B

On a piece of paper, group the details that go with the main-idea sentence you wrote on page 23. Circle the details that go together, or draw a cluster diagram.

Check your answers on page 182–183.

Drafting

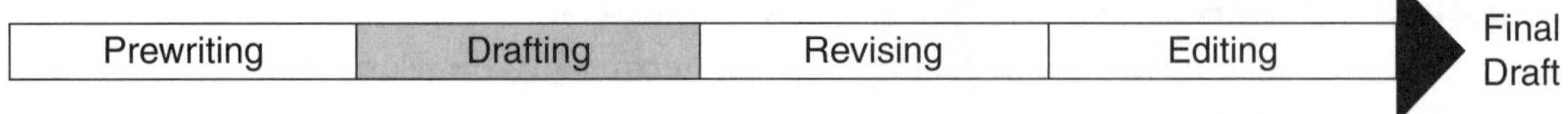

You have practiced all the steps in prewriting. Your writing plan is now complete. You are ready to begin the second stage of the writing process—**drafting**, or writing a first version.

The first version of an essay is called the **first draft**. The purpose of this draft is to get your ideas on paper in essay form. The first draft will probably be somewhat rough and unpolished. It may have spelling errors or other kinds of mistakes. You will have the chance to improve and correct the draft later in the writing process when you revise and edit.

Drafting from a Plan

As you write your first draft, follow the plan you created during prewriting. This example shows step-by-step how to write from a plan. (You may notice a few spelling errors and other mistakes in the sample first draft. You can correct them later.)

Step 1: Build an introduction around the main-idea sentence.

Sometimes the main idea is stated in the first sentence of an essay. Often, however, the introduction of an essay begins with an interesting sentence or two. These sentences help get the reader's attention. They lead the reader to the main idea. Then the introduction ends with the main-idea sentence.

Writing Plan	Sample First Draft
Main-Idea Sentence	**Introduction**
Here are some ways to lose those extra pounds.	Are you tired of being overwieght? Would you like to look and feel better? Here are some ways to lose those extra pounds.

Step 2: Write the body of your essay, using the details in your groups or clusters.
Turn each group or cluster into a paragraph.

Cluster 1

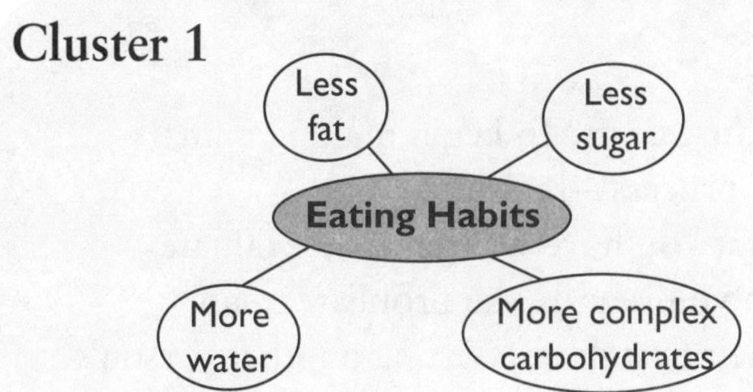

First Paragraph of Body

Begin by building good eating habits. Like drinking plenty of water. Stay away from sugary and fatty foods. Instead, eat foods that are high in complex carbohydrates.

Cluster 2

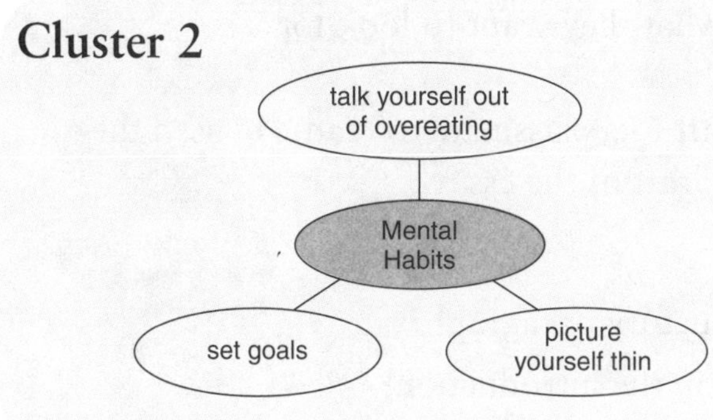

Second Paragraph of Body

It is also important to develop good mental habits. Each week set a realisitic weight-loss goal. That way, you have something specific to aim for. When your tempted to overeat, talk yourself out of it. Picture the thin person inside yourself just waiting to get out.

Step 3: Build a conclusion around a restatement of the main idea.
Write a few sentences leading to your restatement. Then end with the restatement.

Main-Idea Sentence

Here are some good ways to lose those extra pounds.

Conclusion

Losing weight is not easy. But you can do it if you want to and you know how. When you follow the methods in this essay, you, too, will lose weight.

Exercise 7

On a piece of paper, write the first draft of the essay you planned on page 25.

Check your answers on page 183.

Revising

Prewriting	Drafting	Revising	Editing	Final Draft

You have written a draft of an essay, but it is a first draft. To begin making a final draft, work through the third stage of the writing process—revising.

When you **revise**, you take a second look at what you have written. You evaluate your essay to see how it might be improved. Then you rewrite the problem areas.

Many writers like to have someone else read their first draft. Getting another person's opinion can be very helpful. No matter how careful you are, it is easy to overlook problems in your own essay. Many writers also find it helpful to use a checklist when they revise. A checklist helps them keep track of what they want to look for.

The writer of the weight-loss essay gave her draft to a classmate to read. He used the following Revision Checklist to evaluate the first draft of the essay.

Yes	No	
☑	❑	1. Does the essay have an introductory paragraph?
☑	❑	2. Is the main idea clearly stated in the introduction?
☑	❑	3. Does the body contain at least one paragraph?
❑	☑	4. Does the body contain enough details to develop the main idea?
☑	❑	5. Do all the details in the body support the main idea?
☑	❑	6. Are the details in the body logically organized?
☑	❑	7. Is there a paragraph of conclusion?
☑	❑	8. Does the conclusion restate the main idea?
❑	☑	9. Are all the sentences and ideas clear?

Notice that the evaluator felt the body needed further development. He suggested that the writer add something about exercise, because exercise is an important part of weight loss. In addition, the evaluator pointed out some ideas that were not clear. For example, the writer said that dieters should drink "plenty" of water. But she did not say why or how much. The writer's revisions are on the next page.

Take It Off!

Are you tired of being overwieght? Would you like to look and feel better? Here are some ways to lose those extra pounds.

at least five glasses of water a day. Water will help cut your appetite.

Begin by building good eating habits. Like drinking ^ ~~plenty of water~~. ^ *s* Stay away from

In addition,

sugary and fatty foods. Instead, eat foods that are high in complex carbohydrates. ^

such as potatoes or pasta.

Its also important to develop good mental habits. Each week set a realisitic weight-loss goal. ^ The goal will give you something specific to aim for. When your tempted to

For example, say you'll try to lose one pound.

overeat, talk yourself out of it. Picture the thin person inside yourself just waiting to get out. *You should also try to exercise each day. Walk instead of driving. Climb the stairs instead of using the elevator.*

Losing weight is not easy. But you can do it if you want to and you know how. When you follow the methods in this essay, you, too, will lose weight.

Exercise 8

PART A

Answer the questions on the Revision Checklist to evaluate the following essay.

Just One Job?

After I graduated from high school, I went right to work. Now I am a secretary for three lawyers.

I do the work of many people. When I enter letters and legal papers on the computer, I am a word processor. When I correct the lawyers' spelling and grammar mistakes, I do the work of an English teacher. I am a travel agent when I make plane and hotel reservations for my bosses. I am a mental health worker when I listen to their problems and offer advice.

PART B

Answer the questions on the Revision Checklist to evaluate the first draft you wrote for Exercise 7.

Check your answer on page 183.

Editing

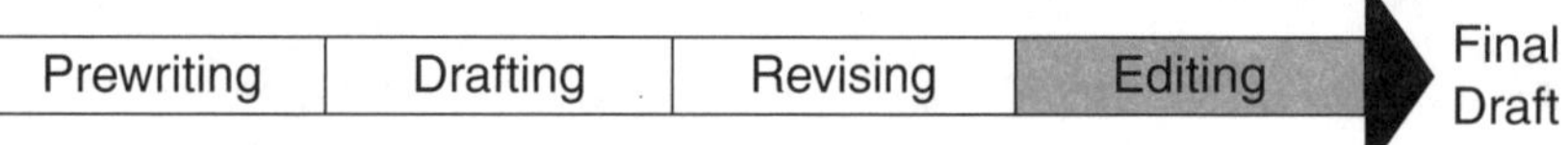

LANGUAGE Tip

Computers can help you proofread, but they cannot do the work for you. If you use the wrong word, the computer may not know that. Reading aloud and having a friend help you are two good ways to proofread.

The last stage of the writing process is editing. When you **edit**, you find and correct mistakes in grammar, mechanics, and usage. Edit the revised draft of "Take It Off!" on page 29. Find and correct five errors in the essay. Then check your answers on page 183.

Were you able to find all the errors? If you are like most student writers, you need to review grammar, mechanics, and usage. Part II of this book explains the areas that often trouble student writers. If you need help with a point of grammar, look it up in the table of contents. The table of contents will tell you which page to study in Part II.

This book also gives you a chance to do a more complete review. By doing the Editing Exercises at the end of chapters 2–6, you will review five major areas: nouns, pronouns, verbs, adjectives and adverbs, and sentence structure.

Editing Exercise: Nouns

Underline and correct the noun error in each sentence.

Dear Reba,

I received your letter in this mornings mail. It certainly brightened a chilly monday. It's always great to hear from my favorite Aunt.

We've had an unusually cold Fall this year. An early september frost took us by surprise. Most peoples gardens were ruined. You should have seen my poor tomatos! On the other hand, the leafs are especially colorful this year.

Bo and Nedra are really looking forward to halloween. Kids costumes were on sale, so I bought new ghost outfits. This year we're going trick-or-treating with a few other familys. It will be easier on me and more fun for the childrens.

It's getting late and I have to pack tomorrow's lunchs, so I'll sign off for now.

Love,
Marcella

Check your answer on page 183.

Chapter 3

Test Skill

Describing

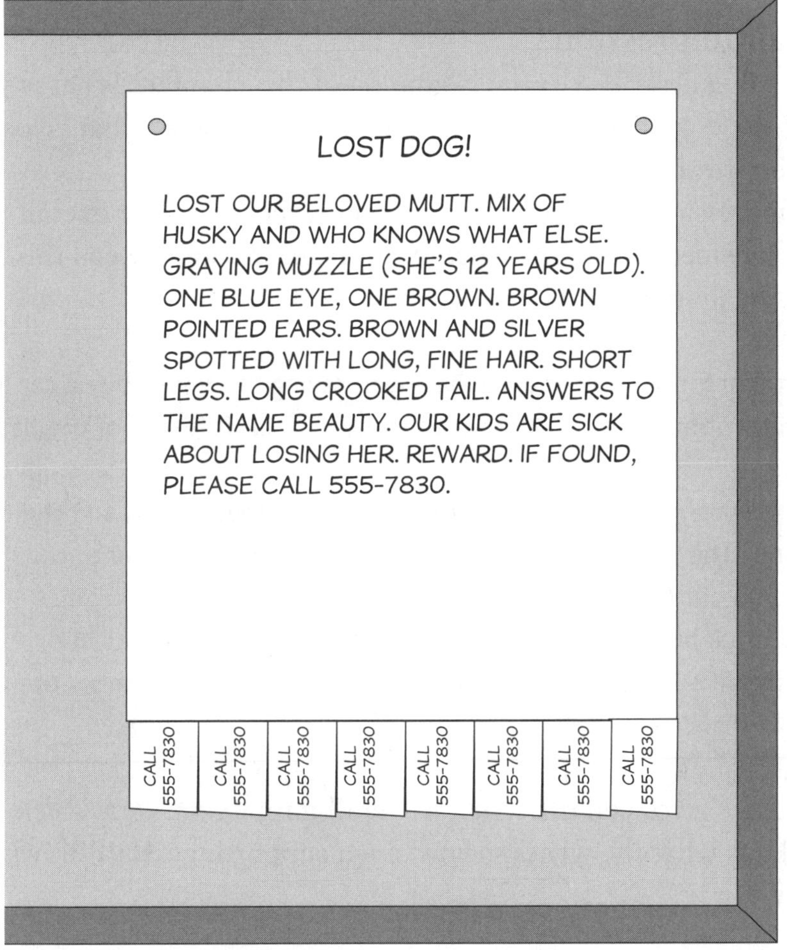
LOST DOG!
LOST OUR BELOVED MUTT. MIX OF HUSKY AND WHO KNOWS WHAT ELSE. GRAYING MUZZLE (SHE'S 12 YEARS OLD). ONE BLUE EYE, ONE BROWN. BROWN POINTED EARS. BROWN AND SILVER SPOTTED WITH LONG, FINE HAIR. SHORT LEGS. LONG CROOKED TAIL. ANSWERS TO THE NAME BEAUTY. OUR KIDS ARE SICK ABOUT LOSING HER. REWARD. IF FOUND, PLEASE CALL 555-7830.
CALL 555-7830
CALL 555-7830
CALL 555-7830
CALL 555-7830
CALL 555-7830
CALL 555-7830
CALL 555-7830
CALL 555-7830

This notice describes a family's pet dog. You have probably seen similar notices hanging in store windows or on lamp posts. The notice contains a good description. The owner wants to make sure that people will recognize the dog.

Skill in describing comes in handy. In this chapter, you will learn how to write good descriptions.

After working through this chapter, you should be able to

- identify the overall impression (or main idea) of a description
- write descriptive details
- organize descriptive details, using space order
- prewrite, draft, revise, and edit your own description

Elements of Descriptive Essays

Reread the notice at the beginning of this chapter. Like any good description, it contains three key elements. It gives readers a clear overall impression. It includes many specific details. And it is organized in a way that makes it easy to picture what is being described.

Main Idea: Overall Impression

Can you picture the dog described at the beginning of this chapter? What is your overall impression of the dog? Do you imagine a funny-looking mutt that is loved by its family? That **overall impression** is the main idea of the description.

Often the overall impression is stated in the main-idea sentence. The overall impression is usually included in the introduction to the description. Read this excerpt from a descriptive essay about a car. The main idea is underlined.

For more than two years, my brother Jerry has been saving money to buy a car. Last Saturday, he finally bought one. The car is quite a beauty. In fact, <u>it is one of the flashiest cars you will ever see.</u>

Outside, the car is bright red with polished trim. The roof slopes back, and the bottom rides low to the ground. The whole car has a fast, sleek look. It is the kind of car that makes police officers pull out their radar guns.

Inside, you will find black bucket seats. The dashboard has so many lights and instruments that it looks like it belongs in a spacecraft. The instruments show the world that this is a high-performance car.

The main-idea sentence gives you the writer's overall impression: *Jerry's new car is flashy.* The body explains what the writer means. Each supporting detail shows that the car is, indeed, a flashy car.

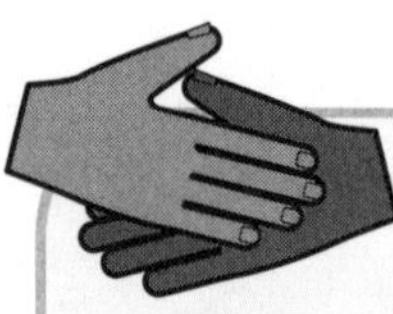

With a Partner

Look for descriptions of cars in dealers' booklets or in magazines. Read the descriptions carefully. Together, decide on the overall impression that the writers want to give you of each car.

Exercise 1

Read the descriptions below. Then circle the letter of the sentence that describes the overall impression created by each description.

Description 1

My friend's newborn was as wrinkled as a prune. Its head was funny-shaped. Its face was scratched. Its eyes and mouth were all squished up. It held its fists shut tightly while it kicked its skinny legs. Then I realized this was my best friend's baby. Suddenly the baby became a beautiful little human being.

(a) The baby was the most beautiful newborn I had ever seen.

(b) At first the baby looked ugly and wrinkled.

Description 2

You can easily recognize our house. That is because it is the coziest-looking home on the block. From the street, you walk up a flat stone path to a screened-in porch with a swing. The house is painted gray, and the shutters are white. Each window has a flowerbox filled with petunias. Outside the front door is a mat that says "Welcome."

(a) The house looks old and run-down.

(b) The house is homey and old-fashioned.

Description 3

My favorite lake is in a wooded area in Georgia. From the shore, I can look out onto a peaceful scene. To the left, a narrow inlet cuts back into the pine forest. In the middle of the lake, a large headland juts out of the water. Red bluffs rise up from the blue water. Off to the right, the lake reflects the hills. These hills stretch as far as I can see.

(a) The lake is beautiful and peaceful.

(b) The lake has a narrow inlet on the left.

Check your answers on page 183.

Developing the Main Idea: Descriptive Details

How does a writer create a picture in the reader's mind? The writer uses **descriptive details**. To be descriptive, a detail must appeal to one of the five senses: sight, hearing, taste, smell, or touch. In other words, a descriptive detail must help you imagine how something looks, sounds, tastes, smells, or feels.

"Sight words" are especially important in a description. Sight words tell the color, size, or shape of something. For example, look back at the lost-dog notice, on page 31. These words help you "see" the dog in your mind:

- graying muzzle
- one blue eye, one brown
- pointed brown ears
- brown with silver spots
- long, fine hair
- short legs
- long crooked tail

Look back at the paragraph about Jerry's new car, on page 32. What words and phrases help you picture the car? You probably noticed these descriptive words:

- bright red
- polished trim
- roof slopes
- low to the ground
- fast
- sleek
- black bucket seats
- dashboard . . . in a spacecraft

The appearance of the dog and the car is important. As a result, the two descriptions appeal to the sense of sight. But in other cases, a writer might want to appeal to a different sense.

For example, what if you were describing dinner at an Italian restaurant? You might describe the aroma of oregano and tomatoes. You might describe the spicy flavor of Italian sausage. Or you might describe the crunch of the bread and the sting of the hot cheese.

When you write a description, think about the senses you most want to appeal to. Make your readers see, hear, taste, smell, or feel what you are describing.

In Your Journal

Draw lines to make a five-column chart. At the top of each column, write one of the five senses: sight, hearing, taste, smell, touch. Visit (or recall visiting) a crowded fast-food restaurant. Brainstorm about the sights, sounds, tastes, smells, and feelings. Write down as many descriptive details as you can for each of the senses.

Exercise 2

Complete the paragraph by adding descriptive details.

Each spring when I was a child, a traveling carnival would come to town. I loved visiting it. My favorite ride was the ________________. If I close my eyes, I can still picture it. It was ____

____

____

What did it feel like to be on the ride? It was ________________________________

____

____

Food stands filled the air with tempting aromas such as ____________________________

____

____

I always bought __________ to eat. It tasted ______________________________________

____

____

As I walked around the carnival, I could hear the sounds of ________________________

____

____

Check your answers on page 184.

Organizing Ideas: Space Order

Think of a jigsaw puzzle. Its pieces contain all the details needed to create a whole picture. But if the pieces are set in the wrong place, they create nothing but jumble.

The same is true of descriptive details in an essay. If you are not careful about how you organize them, you will create a jumble. Your reader will have a hard time picturing what you are describing. But if you follow space order, you will create a complete picture. When you put details in **space order**, you organize them in the order that you see them or experience them.

The description of the Georgia lake, on page 33, is organized **from left to right**. Each detail describes a part of the lake. The writer helps the reader picture the scene by describing the details as he sees them when his eyes move across the lake.

Main Idea →	My favorite fishing lake is in a wooded area in Georgia.
Detail 1 →	To the left, . . .
Detail 2 →	In the middle of the lake, . . .
Detail 3 →	Off to the right, . . .

Space order can also be organized **from top to bottom** or **from head to toe** (or tail). That is the order the dog owner followed in the description of the dog, on page 31.

Sometimes space order is organized **from outside to inside**. This is the order the writer used to describe his brother's new car, on page 32. Another way of describing is **from far away to close up**. This is the way the writer organized the description of the house on page 33.

Of course, if you want to, you can reverse any of the orders—for example, you can organize details from close up to far away or from inside to outside.

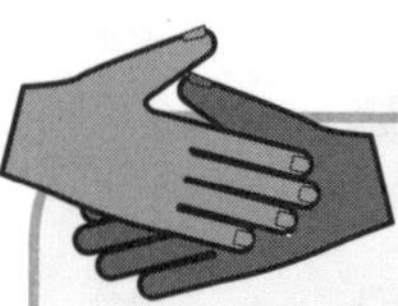

With a Partner

Write a short description of something without naming what you are describing. Give your description to your partner. See whether your partner can guess what you have described. Then switch roles. Read your partner's description and try to guess what is being described.

Exercise 3

Tell how each paragraph is organized:

from left to right
from outside to inside
from far away to close up

1. The heart-shaped box was beautiful. It was covered in bright red satin and adorned with gold lace. The letters on the lid said "To My Darling." I lifted the lid, and there were a dozen hand-dipped chocolates. Each chocolate sat is a lacy red paper.

   Order: ______________________________

2. From the plane, the countryside looked like a patchwork quilt. Cars the size of ants crawled down roads no wider than ribbons. As we began to descend, my point of view changed. The patches became cornfields. The ant-like cars grew bigger as the roads grew wider.

   Order: ______________________________

3. It was the messiest room I had ever seen. To my left was an unmade bed. Sheets and blankets lay knotted on top of it. In the middle of the floor was a cardboard pizza box. It was smeared with oil and littered with half-chewed crusts. To my right was a mountain of dirty jeans and T-shirts.

   Order: ______________________________

Check your answers on page 184.

In Your Journal

Write a description of your favorite room in your home. Be sure to include plenty of sight words. Use space order to organize the details in your description. Describe the room from left to right.

Read a Descriptive Essay

You have studied three elements of description: overall impression, descriptive details, and space order. Look for these elements as you read this descriptive essay.

In this essay, the writer describes a place she visited. As you read the description, try to picture what it is like to arrive somewhere that you have never been before.

One Night at a Bed-and-Breakfast

(1) I love to travel. However, I do not always enjoy staying at ordinary motels. You know the kind, located just off noisy main highways. Their rooms are all the same. They have two double beds, a double dresser, a TV, and a no-frills bathroom. There is nothing special about them. But I recently had the pleasure of staying in a much more interesting and memorable place—a bed-and-breakfast.

(2) To get to the B&B, I drove through a quaint little town. Large shade trees formed an orange-and-yellow canopy above my car. On both sides of the road were old houses with big front porches.

(3) I soon arrived at a large house that looked like the picture I had seen on-line. The address matched the one I was looking for. On the front porch were a swing, a wrought-iron table, four chairs, and a friendly looking carved pumpkin.

(4) I shuffled through piles of crunchy dry leaves to reach the porch. As I climbed the steps, I spotted a note taped to the front door. It said, "Welcome to the River

Lodge. I have gone on an errand. Please take your bags to the room on the third floor. I will see you when I get back." I tried the door, and it swung open. No lock? I was amazed.

(5) I stepped into the house and set my bag down on an oriental rug in a cozy parlor. The pleasant smell of apples and spices welcomed me. To the right of the door was an old roll-top desk next to a grandfather clock. In the far right corner was a bookcase filled with books and small **knickknacks.**[1] Straight ahead was a steep staircase. To my left was the entry into the living room.

LANGUAGE Tip

B&Bs began in the 1800s when travelers needed a safe place to sleep and a good breakfast. Most B&Bs are very small. They are often in private homes. Some are located in unusual places such as lighthouses and old jails.

(6) As I hauled my suitcase up two flights of stairs, I wished I had packed lighter. But when I reached my room, I decided that my effort to reach the third floor had been worthwhile. The room was like something out of a storybook. Its queen-sized bed was covered by a white quilt embroidered with soft-pink flowers. Across from the bed was a small antique dresser. Beside it sat an **ornate**[2] wooden cupboard. On each side of the room were two tall windows that let in the last rays of the sunset. In the bathroom, a soft terry-cloth robe hung on a hook. I noticed a tiny dish filled with fragrant soaps and lotions.

(7) When I heard the front door open and then slam closed, I walked downstairs to meet the owner of the B&B. She greeted me warmly. The innkeeper looked exactly the way I had thought she would look. Her gray hair was rolled up in a bun on the back of her head. She was dressed casually, in jeans and a sweatshirt. She took a few minutes to show me around the rest of the house. She begin in the dining room, filled with heavy, dark furniture. When we moved into the kitchen, I was surprised to see modern stainless-steel appliances, so different from the furnishings in the rest of the house.

(8) Back upstairs in my room, I snuggled under the warm quilt to read a book. The next thing I knew, it was morning and I was waking up to the aroma of coffee brewing.

(9) My breakfast was wonderful! Who wouldn't enjoy freshly squeezed orange juice, hot coffee, and a fruit cup filled with sweet pineapple chunks, halved grapes, and juicy melon slices? The main course was my favorite—pancakes covered with sliced apples and swimming in maple syrup. The food tasted as good as it looked!

(10) Now I am spoiled. No motel can match the comfort and friendliness I found at the bed-and-breakfast. Why should I settle for a dull motel when I can enjoy the unique experience of a B&B?

---

[1]**knickknacks:** small objects, often displayed on shelves or in cases

[2]**ornate:** fancy; decorated with elaborate carvings

Check Your Understanding

PART A

Circle the answer to each question about "One Night at a Bed-and-Breakfast." Look back at the essay if you need to.

1. What is the writer's overall impression of the bed-and-breakfast?
   (a) It's a better choice than a motel.
   (b) Bed-and-breakfasts are found in out-of-the way locations.
2. Which senses does the writer appeal to in paragraph 4?
   (a) hearing and sight
   (b) sight and smell
3. Which senses does the writer appeal to in paragraph 6?
   (a) hearing, sight, and taste
   (b) sight, touch, and smell
4. How does the writer organize the description of the room in paragraph 5?
   (a) from right to left
   (b) from top to bottom

PART B

For each of the following senses, list at least two descriptive details from the essay.

1. sight: ______________________________

   ____

2. sound: ______________________________

   ____

3. smell: ______________________________

   ____

4. taste: ______________________________

   ____

5. touch: ______________________________

   ____

Check your answers on page 184.

Write a Descriptive Essay

Prewriting: Selecting a Topic and a Purpose

In "One Night at a Bed-and-Breakfast," the author describes a place that is special to her. **Write a descriptive essay about a place, a person, or a possession that's special to you.** Your purpose is to describe. The topic you choose to describe could be

- an outdoor scene
- a prized possession
- a person
- yourself

Below are some ideas to get you started. Choose *one* of these topics or use a topic of your own. Check your journal for ideas. You may have written about something or someone that you would enjoy describing in an essay.

- a private place where you go when you need to be alone
- an exciting place, such as an amusement park
- a relaxing place, such as a lake
- something special you own, such as a car or a ring
- your husband or wife, boyfriend or girlfriend
- your child
- what you see when you look in the mirror

Write your topic here.

Topic: ____

Prewriting: Developing Your Topic

Now that you have your topic, you need to think of details so you can develop the topic. One excellent way to think of descriptive details is to observe the person or thing you are describing. Observing is a special kind of brainstorming.

When you observe, you look at your subject from every angle. You note details such as color, size, and shape. You think of how your subject involves your other senses, such as touch or smell. Then you list each detail.

Here are the notes a student wrote. The topic of his description was the view from his front porch.

Sights	Sounds	Smells
white frame house	honking horns	stink of diesel fumes
brown brick factory	squealing brakes	
smokestacks	blaring car radios	
skyscrapers		
steel and glass		

Carefully observe the person or thing you chose to describe. If you cannot observe your subject, picture the person or thing in your mind.

On the lines below, make an observation chart like the one above. Write down as many descriptive details as you can.

Prewriting: Organizing Your Ideas

Finish prewriting by organizing your ideas.

Write a main-idea sentence.

Ask yourself, "What overall impression do my descriptive details make?"

Main-idea sentence: ____

____

Group your descriptive details.

Decide whether you need one, two, or more paragraphs for the body of your essay. Draw a line around the details that go together. Or, if you prefer, draw clusters showing how the details go together.

Decide what order to put your details in.

Do you want to describe a person from head to toe? An object from the outside to the inside? A place from left to right or from far away to close up?

The student who made the observation chart on page 42 chose to organize his details from close up to far away.

Write the type of order you will use for your essay.

Order: ____

Many writers find it is helpful to draw a sketch of the space order they plan to use. Try drawing a sketch, if you wish. Follow the student's example.

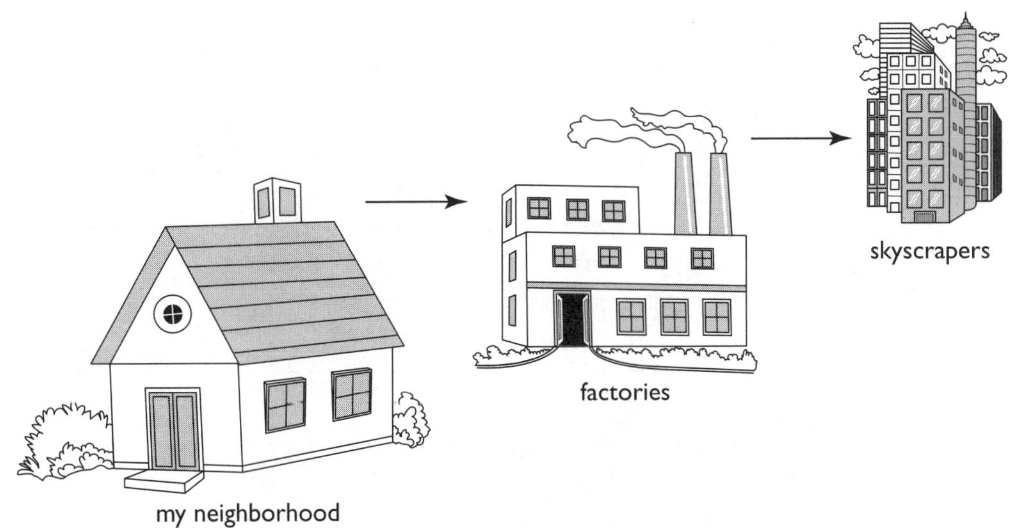

Drafting

The next stage of the writing process is drafting. During this stage, you use your prewriting plan to write a first draft. Remember that a first draft is just a first try. You will have a chance to improve your writing when you revise and edit.

Using your prewriting plan, write a first draft on the topic of your choice. If you need more space, continue writing on a piece of paper.

Write an introduction. Include a main-idea sentence.

Use descriptive details in the body.

Write a conclusion that restates the main idea.

Revising

The next stage is to evaluate your first draft. You may do this alone or with a partner. First, do the Revision Warm-Up. Then use the Revision Checklist to revise your draft.

Revision Warm-Up

Evaluate the student's first draft by answering each question on the Revision Checklist.

The View from My Front Porch

After a long, hot day at work, I like to sit on my front porch with something cool to drink.

White frame houses line my block. We moved to our home last summer. Horns honk, bus brakes squeal, and the diesel fumes stink. But then the neighborhood quiets down. The brown brick walls of factories rise several stories above the homes. Smokestacks rise even higher above the factory roofs. Smoke swirls out of one. It rises from another. The downtown skyscrapers line up along the horizon. These glass and steel giants create the city's skyline. Their windows reflect the sun's golden setting rays.

Soon thousands of small white city lights will replace the day, and the kids will drive by with their radios blaring.

☑ Revision Checklist

Yes	No	
❑	❑	1. Does the essay have an introductory paragraph?
❑	❑	2. Is the overall impression stated in a main-idea sentence?
❑	❑	3. Does the body contain at least one paragraph?
❑	❑	4. Do all the descriptive details support the overall impression?
❑	❑	5. Does the body contain enough descriptive details to develop the overall impression?
❑	❑	6. Are the details in the body arranged in a logical space order?
❑	❑	7. Is there a paragraph of conclusion?
❑	❑	8. Does the conclusion restate the main idea?
❑	❑	9. Are all the sentences and ideas clear?

Check your answers on page 184.

Editing

The last stage of the writing process is editing. During this stage, you look for and correct errors in grammar, mechanics, and usage.

Do the Editing Exercise. Then edit the draft of your essay. Look for and correct noun and pronoun errors as well as other errors. If possible, work with a partner.

Editing Exercise: Pronouns

Underline and correct the nine pronoun errors in the letter.

Dear Linn,

Its too bad you couldn't make it to our New Year's Eve party. Glenn and myself missed having you.

About twenty of our friends showed up. As usual, the Nielands brought they're kids. I usually love children, but the Nieland kids are so loud! They gave Glenn and I a headache. The Smiths sort of invited theirselves. However, we didn't really mind. We enjoyed having them.

We decorated the living room with the silver streamers and balloons that you gave to we. Glenn and me put the long table on the right side of the living room. It was loaded with all kinds of food. Everyone loved Glenn's version of potato salad. Mine's was less popular. However, them pizza puffs I made were gobbled up fast.

We're already beginning to plan next year's party, and we hope you can come. Put it on your calendar now!

Love,
Juanita

Check your answers on page 184.

Chapter 4

Test Skill

Narrating

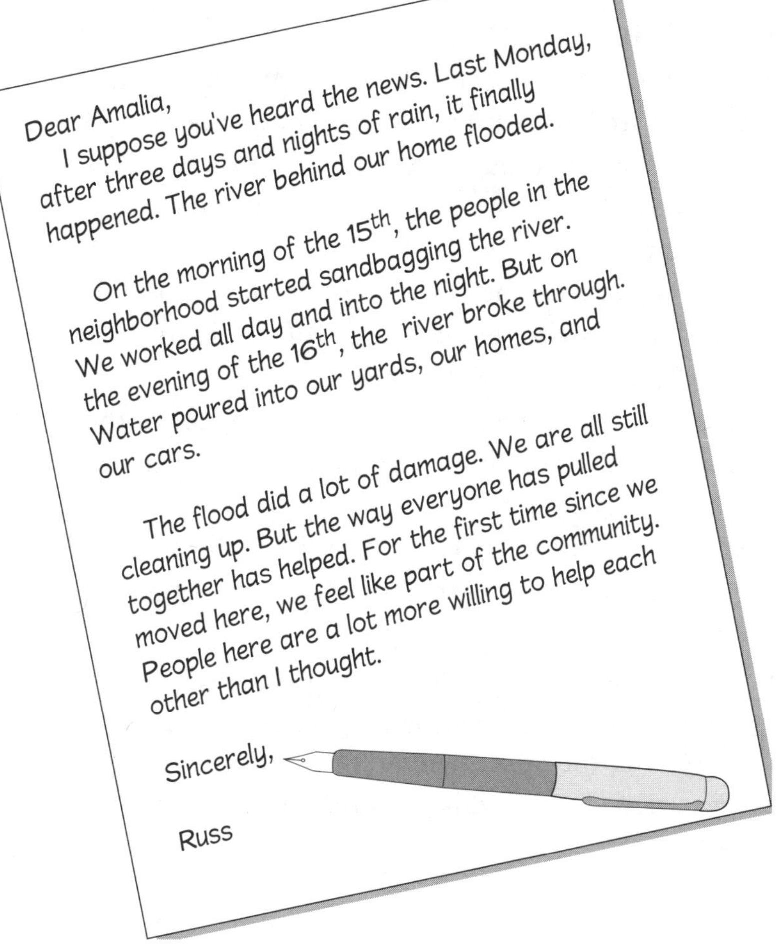
Dear Amalia,

I suppose you've heard the news. Last Monday, after three days and nights of rain, it finally happened. The river behind our home flooded.

On the morning of the 15th, the people in the neighborhood started sandbagging the river. We worked all day and into the night. But on the evening of the 16th, the river broke through. Water poured into our yards, our homes, and our cars.

The flood did a lot of damage. We are all still cleaning up. But the way everyone has pulled together has helped. For the first time since we moved here, we feel like part of the community. People here are a lot more willing to help each other than I thought.

Sincerely,

Russ

The letter above is a **personal narrative**—the story of a person's experiences. Personal narratives are a familiar kind of writing. You have written a personal narrative if you have ever written a letter about a family event or a postcard about a trip. In this chapter, you will learn more about writing narratives.

After working through this chapter, you should be able to

- find the main idea of a personal narrative
- identify three kinds of conflicts
- use time order to organize ideas
- prewrite, draft, revise, and edit a personal narrative

Elements of Personal Narratives

In many ways, the letter at the beginning of this chapter is a typical personal narrative. The meaning of the story is summed up at the end. The story tells about a conflict. Events are told about in the order in which they happened. In this section, you will take a closer look at these three elements of narration.

Main Idea: Lesson in Life

Personal experiences often teach us lessons about life. When something unusual happens, we may change our attitude toward a person or a situation. Or we may discover something about ourselves, about others, or about the world. This lesson about life is very often the main idea of a narrative. It is the point that writers want to make when they tell about their experiences.

Reread the letter about the flood. What is the point of the narrative? If you are not sure, ask yourself, "What did the writer learn because of the flood?" The writer learned that his neighbors were willing to help one another.

Where does the writer make this statement? He states this idea in the last few sentences of his letter. Telling the meaning of what happened is a good way to conclude the story.

You have learned that it is usually a good idea to write your main-idea statement in the introduction. Personal narratives, however, often save the main idea for the last. This is one way that personal narratives are a little different from other kinds of essays. In many cases, the writer uses the first few sentences of the essay to "set the stage." The writer often describes the situation in which the personal experience took place.

Look again at the letter about the flood. The first paragraph sets the stage by letting you know that a flood occurred. The flood is the situation in which the writer learned the truth about his neighbors.

In Your Journal

Each of the following sayings could be the main idea of a narrative. Select one saying, and write a story to go along with it. Make the saying the last sentence of your story.

- **Look before you leap.**
- **You can't judge a book by its cover.**
- **Absence makes the heart grow fonder.**

Exercise 1

PART A

Underline the main-idea sentence in each personal narrative.

We heard the tornado watch announced on the radio. But we did not pay much attention to it. Then we noticed a funnel cloud way off on the hill. Lisa and I grabbed the kids and headed for the basement. At first it sounded like a huge train coming toward us. Then the swirling winds hit. Smash! Within seconds, our house was destroyed. I was in shock. All that we had worked for was gone. However, I was thankful we were alive. As I hugged my wife and kids, I thought about what really matters to me.

Three killings in our neighborhood proved that the gangs had gotten out of hand. One of the dead was a two-year-old girl. That was when some neighborhood people decided to fight back. One night we gathered together in the office of our city council member. We decided to "take back the streets." From then on, neighbors would leave their porch lights on. We would stay outside as much as possible. If we saw a problem, we would contact the police, and we would cooperate with them. We would prove that people working together can get rid of gangs.

PART B

Circle the letter of the best main-idea sentence to use at the end of this narrative.

There I stood—at the edge of the pool. Everyone else was enjoying the cool water, but I was scared. I had been afraid of water all my life. Now, however, I was determined to overcome that fear. I held my nose, shut my eyes, and jumped. At first the water closing over my head terrified me, but soon my feet touched bottom. I quickly pushed myself up. When I reached the surface, I grabbed the edge of the pool and floated. I had done it!

(a) I had stood at the edge of the pool and jumped in.

(b) I realized that it is foolish to let fear rule your life.

Check your answers on page 184.

Developing the Main Idea: Conflict

Often people learn a lesson in life when they face a **conflict**—a problem or struggle. For that reason, many personal narratives tell the story of a conflict. Conflict captures people's interest and holds it. Think of a TV show or movie that you recently saw and liked. What problems did the people face? Did you wonder how the people would solve their problems? Conflict builds suspense in the minds of viewers (and readers). It makes them wonder what will happen next.

There are three main kinds of conflicts:

- person against person
- person against nature
- person against self

If you understand the three kinds of conflict, you'll become a better reader as well as a better writer of narratives.

Person Against Person This kind of conflict happens when people disagree or when they compete with one another. For example, an argument between a husband and wife is a person-against-person conflict. The tension between salespeople trying to outsell one another to earn a bonus is also a conflict.

Person Against Nature This kind of conflict involves problems caused by natural disasters. The letter at the beginning of this chapter tells about a person-against-nature conflict: neighbors fighting against a flood. Fires, storms, and diseases are other examples of natural disasters that can cause person-against-nature conflicts.

Person Against Self This kind of conflict involves a struggle within a person. For example, a woman who is torn between having children or having a career is in a person-against-self conflict. A man struggling to break a gambling habit is another example of this kind of conflict.

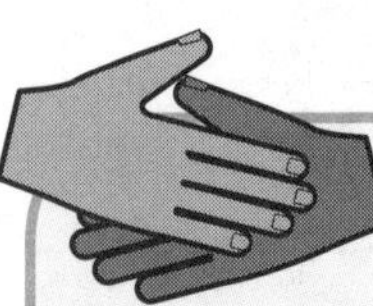

With a Partner

Look at the front page of a newspaper. Read the headline and the first paragraph of each story. How many stories involve conflict? With your partner, decide which kind of conflict is described in each story.

Exercise 2

PART A

Match each example with the correct kind of conflict.

_____	**1.** the Bears against the Lions	(**a**) person against person
_____	**2.** a woman trying not to drink	(**b**) person against nature
_____	**3.** a pilot landing in thick fog	(**c**) person against self

PART B

Write the kind of conflict each paragraph is about.

1. I did not know what to do. On the one hand, I knew I would be happier living apart from Al. On the other, I could not bear to separate the kids from their dad.

   ____

2. Thank God it was over. It had been a tough fire to fight. The freezing weather had made it even tougher. Two men were badly hurt.

   ____

3. I had gone almost 24 hours without sleep. My boss had given me yet another impossible deadline. I was doing the best I could. But once again, it was not good enough for him. When he walked over and asked for the report, I told him I was not finished writing it. "That's it!" he roared. "You're fired!" Angrily I replied, "You can't fire me because I quit!"

   ____

Check your answers on page 185.

In Your Journal

Think about conflicts that you've faced in your life. Brainstorm to make three lists—one for each kind of conflict. List as many conflicts as you can for each list.

Organizing Ideas: Time Order

When you tell a story, you usually tell the events in the order in which they happened. You begin by talking about what happened first, then what happened next, and so on. This organization of ideas is called **time order**. Time order is an excellent way to organize a personal narrative.

Read the following paragraph, which is *not* written in time order. Is it easy to understand what happened?

> The day I graduated, everything seemed to go wrong. On the way to school, our car got a flat tire. We ended up arriving ten minutes after the ceremony had started. When I went to pick up my suit, the cleaners could not find it. I had to borrow my brother's suit, which was too big. I woke up with a sore throat and a fever. Worst of all, I tripped as I walked across the stage.

All the events are included in the paragraph. However, the story is difficult to follow. That is because the events are not in the order in which they occurred. See what happens when the narrative is written in time order.

> The day I graduated, everything seemed to go wrong. First, I woke up with a sore throat and a fever. Then, when I went to pick up my suit, the cleaners could not find it. I had to borrow my brother's suit, which was too big. On the way to school, our car got a flat tire. We ended up arriving ten minutes after the ceremony had started. Last but not least, I tripped as I walked across the stage.

In Your Journal

Describe an exciting play you watched at a recent sporting event. Tell about the play in detail. Put the events in time order.

Exercise 3

Put each list of events in time order. Number the first event 1, the second event 2, and so on.

1. _____ The doctor told me I had diabetes.

   _____ I had to go through tests to see what was wrong.

   _____ I hadn't been feeling right for months.

   _____ I decided to go see the doctor.

   _____ I am watching my diet and taking shots, so I feel great.

2. _____ All ten pins fell—a strike!

   _____ I had to get a strike to beat my old bowling rival.

   _____ The ball crashed into the lead pin.

   _____ The ball rolled down the lane.

   _____ I swung my arm forward and let the ball fly.

3. _____ The agency gave me a list of job openings.

   _____ I found a position as a sales associate.

   _____ I went to our city's employment office.

   _____ I was laid off from my job.

4. _____ I went to the station to identify the suspect.

   _____ I heard footsteps on my front porch late at night.

   _____ The police chased a prowler through my backyard.

   _____ I called the police.

   _____ The officers cornered and caught the prowler.

Check your answers on page 185.

Read a Personal Narrative

You've studied three elements of description: the lesson-about-life main idea, conflict, and time order. Look for these elements as you read this descriptive essay.

People often remember embarrassing events for many years. Notice all the details that this writer is able to recall about what happened one day when he was a teenager.

A Lesson Learned at the Pool

As a boy, I was shy. My shyness grew worse as I approached my teen years. I hated the idea of people paying attention to me. I was sure that everyone was judging me. Even hanging out with my friends was difficult. I didn't want any of them to notice my mistakes. I tried to stay in the background, quiet and agreeable. I was always a follower, never a leader.

During the summer I turned 13, my friends and I went to the pool almost every day. We would swim a bit, splash a lot, and play cards during the adult swim periods. Those were the ten-minute breaks at the beginning of each hour when only adults were allowed in the pool. The lifeguards would blow their whistles and call all the kids out of the water.

One day my friends were in the mood to dive from the diving board. Diving was something I was fairly good at, so I was happy to go along with the others. Before each dive, we had to stand in line for what seemed like hours. I tried to make every dive worth the wait. Each time I tried to bounce higher, dive straighter, and plunge deeper under the water.

When I rose to the surface, all I could think of was my next dive. I would swim frantically to the side of the pool and haul myself out. Eagerly I would hurry toward the diving board. After my fourth or fifth turn—wonder of wonders—the line of swimmers waiting to dive had disappeared! I scrambled up the steps, ran onto the board, and dove off. As I flew up in the air, I noticed that the water below was nearly empty of swimmers. All of the sudden, I realized what had happened. The line had disappeared because the adult swim had begun. The whistles must have blown while I was still underwater.

LANGUAGE Tip

Punctuation

Use quotation marks around the exact words that someone says.

When two or more people are having a conversation, begin a new paragraph every time the speaker changes.

As the water rushed up at me, I tried to stop in midair. I didn't want to be the only kid in the pool! Gravity, however, won out. Underwater, I wondered if I could hide there for the entire adult swim. But I couldn't. I came up hugging the side of the pool, hoping I could be invisible.

"Hey, kid!" a lifeguard called. "Out of the pool!"

Red with shame, I pulled myself out. I was sure everyone was staring at me. I hurried to the shower room with my head down. If I didn't see anyone, surely no one would be able to see me. I changed to my street clothes with lightning speed and escaped to the outside world.

I spent the rest of the day wondering what my friends were saying about me. Who would admit to knowing such a complete idiot? I could never go back to the pool again. Maybe in the fall I could transfer to another school.

The following day, however, was the hottest day of the summer. My mother didn't believe me when I said I wanted to stay home. "Nonsense," she insisted. "I'm dropping you and your little sister off at the pool. Watch her so she doesn't drown."

Walking my sister to the baby pool, I expected people to point and laugh at me. Strangely, nobody did. Then one of my friends called to me. "Hey, where did you disappear to yesterday?" Rick asked.

"I went home," I mumbled. "I didn't feel good."

"Were you sick? Was it something **contagious**?"

"No." Rick wouldn't go away. "It was just that . . . After what I did . . ."

"What did you do?"

I finally looked at him. He really didn't know what I had done. How could that be? Hadn't everyone seen it?

"I dived in during adult swim," I admitted.

"Oh, yeah? Did the guards throw you out?"

For the first time, I realized that the guards had done nothing other than remind me of the rule. Maybe it wasn't such a crime. And if Rick knew nothing about what had happened, none of my other friends probably knew about it either. It suddenly occurred to me that the whole world wasn't watching everything I did.

After the incident at the pool, I began to relax. I had discovered that I could make a mistake and still survive. I was no longer afraid that everyone was watching me. Instead, I realized that no one was watching me unless I demanded attention. I began to voice my own opinions. In time, I came out of hiding, and I became the person I chose to be.

---

contagious: can be passed from one person to another; example: a cold

Check Your Understanding

PART A

Answer each question about "A Lesson Learned at the Pool." Look back at the essay if you need to.

1. What kind of conflict takes place in this story? Circle the correct letter.
   (a) person against person
   (b) person against nature
   (c) person against self
2. What is the main idea of the story? Circle the correct letter.
   (a) The teen years are difficult for almost everyone.
   (b) People shouldn't be afraid of making mistakes.
   (c) People who are shy should not go to a swimming pool.
3. In what order do the following events take place? Number the first event 1, the second event 2, and so on.
   _____ The narrator learns that his friend did not notice his mistake.
   _____ After the narrator dives into the pool, he realizes the adult swim has already begun.
   _____ The narrator decides that making a mistake in public is not the end of the world.
   _____ The narrator is happy to see there is no line at the diving board.
   _____ The narrator joins his friends in diving from the diving board.

PART B

Answer each question in a sentence or two.

1. At what point in the story do you first learn about the conflict?

   ____

   ____

2. The narrator ends with these words: "I became the person I chose to be." What qualities do you think he may have developed after this incident?

   ____

   ____

Check your answers on page 185.

Write a Personal Narrative

Prewriting: Selecting a Topic and a Purpose

In "A Lesson Learned at the Pool," the author talks about a conflict he experienced. As a result of the conflict, he discovered something about people and something about himself.

Write your own personal narrative. Write about a conflict that you have experienced. Choose a conflict that taught you something. Your purpose is to tell the story of the conflict. The conflict you choose to describe could be

- between you and another person (or other people)
- caused by nature
- experienced within yourself

Below are some ideas to get you started. Choose *one* of these topics or use a topic of your own. Check your journal for ideas. You may have written about a conflict that you want to write about in an essay. Don't forget to include descriptive details to help your readers picture events.

- an argument with a family member or friend
- a problem with your boss
- a sports competition
- an illness that you have recovered from
- a bad habit you have struggled to break
- a difficult choice you had to make
- a fear you have overcome

Write your topic here.

Topic: ____

Prewriting: Developing Your Topic

Now that you have your topic, you need to think of details so you can develop the topic. Questioning is a good way to get ideas for a personal narrative. (You learned about questioning in Chapter 2.)

Here's how a student used questioning to develop ideas. Her topic was overcoming her fear of flying.

Who? my friend Carlos and me

What? went for a plane ride

Where? in Carlos's plane, over my hometown

When? last month

Why? overcame my fear of flying, was missing out on a promotion

How? pictured myself on the ground, victorious; took deep breaths; relaxed; looked around and began to enjoy myself

On the lines below, list ideas that can help you develop your topic. Follow the student's example and use questioning. Or, if you prefer, use a different method, such as brainstorming or freewriting.

Prewriting: Organizing Your Ideas

Finish prewriting by organizing your ideas.

Write a main-idea sentence.

Ask yourself, "What did I learn as a result of the conflict I'm writing about?"

Main-idea sentence: ____

____

Group your descriptive details.

Decide whether you need one, two, or more paragraphs for the body of your essay. Draw a line around the details that go together. Or, if you prefer, draw clusters showing how the details go together.

Put your supporting details in time order.

An easy way to do this is to number each paragraph and each detail within the paragraph. If you wish, follow the student's example.

What type of order you will use for your essay?

____

①
② My friend Carlos and me
③ Went for a plane ride
④ In Carlos's plane, over my hometown
① Last month

② ② Overcome my fear of flying, ① was missing out on a promotion

③
② Pictured myself on the ground, victorious; ① took deep breaths;
③ relaxed; ④ looked around and began to enjoy myself

Drafting

The next stage of the writing process is drafting. During this stage, you use your prewriting plan to write your first draft. Remember that a first draft is just a first try. You will have a chance to improve your writing when you revise and edit.

Using your prewriting plan, write a first draft on the topic of your choice. If you need more space, continue writing on a piece of paper.

Begin by setting the stage.

Write your story in time order.

Use descriptive details.

Conclude with the main idea.

Revising

The next stage is to evaluate your first draft. You may do this alone or with a partner. First, do the Revision Warm-Up. Then use the Revision Checklist to revise your draft.

Revision Warm-Up

Follow the directions to revise the essay below.

1. There is a sentence in the first paragraph that does not belong there. Draw a line through that sentence.
2. Add descriptive details to paragraph 3. What amazing sights did the writer see?
3. The conclusion doesn't have a main-idea sentence. Add one or two sentences that tell the reader the lesson learned.

Sky High

Last month, I found myself in a place I had never been before. I was high over my hometown in a small plane piloted by my friend Carlos. Carlos and I went to grade school together. I was terrified. My heart was pounding loudly in my ears, and I had closed my eyes so tightly that my forehead hurt. How did I get myself into this? I wondered.

Actually, I knew very well. My fear of flying was keeping me from getting a promotion. I was trying to overcome my fear.

"Are you OK?" Carlos asked. "I guess so," was all I could say. I was so scared that I was having trouble talking. Would I faint? I took a deep breath. Then I pictured myself on the ground, victorious. The thought made me relax. Slowly I opened one eye, then the other. I looked out the window and saw the most amazing sights. To my surprise, I began to enjoy myself.

In no time at all, Carlos, said, "We're landing." As I left the plane, my knees were shaking but my head was clear. ______________________________

____

Check your answers on page 185.

☑ Revision Checklist

Yes	No	
❑	❑	1. Does the essay have an introductory paragraph?
❑	❑	2. Are the events in the body in time order?
❑	❑	3. Are there enough descriptive details to help you picture the events?
❑	❑	4. Are there details or sentences that don't belong?
❑	❑	5. Does the conclusion include a main-idea sentence?
❑	❑	6. Are all the sentences and ideas clear?

Editing

The last stage of the writing process is editing. During this stage, you look for and correct errors in grammar, mechanics, and usage.

Do the Editing Exercise. Then edit the draft of your personal narrative. Look for and correct noun, pronoun, and verb errors as well as other errors. If possible, work with a partner.

Editing Exercise: Verbs

Underline and correct the seven verb errors in the essay.

Back to School

I was really nervous about going back to school. My husband and kids was all for it. But I wasn't so sure. I hate school when I was a teenager. Would I hate it now? I was also afraid that I was too old for school.

Then I run into an old friend. She said that she taking high school classes through the library. She said that going to school was fun. She also said that age don't matter.

Now my friend and I go to class two mornings a week. I am doing very well. I love school. My husband say he is proud of me. My kids is proud too. I never thought I could do so well.

Check your answers on page 185.

Chapter 5

Test Skill

Explaining How

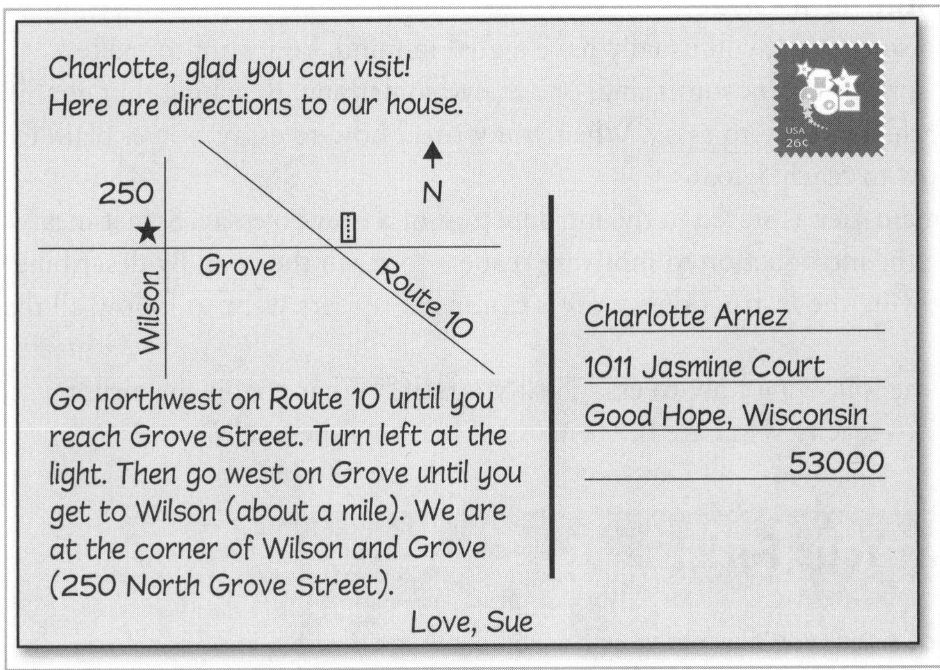

Charlotte, glad you can visit!
Here are directions to our house.
250
N
Grove
Wilson
Route 10
Go northwest on Route 10 until you reach Grove Street. Turn left at the light. Then go west on Grove until you get to Wilson (about a mile). We are at the corner of Wilson and Grove (250 North Grove Street).
Love, Sue
USA 26¢
Charlotte Arnez
1011 Jasmine Court
Good Hope, Wisconsin
53000

This postcard explains how to do something—specifically, how to get to a person's home. "How-to" essays have a similar purpose. They, too, explain how to do something. In this chapter, you will learn how to write a good how-to essay.

After working through this chapter, you should be able to

- find the main idea of a how-to essay
- identify the steps involved in a process
- use time order to organize the steps in a process
- prewrite, draft, revise, and edit your own how-to essay

Elements of How-To Essays

Reread the postcard at the beginning of this chapter. Although instructions are not essays, they have some of the elements of a good how-to essay. Instructions clearly state a goal. They explain how to reach that goal. Instructions should be well organized so they will be easy to follow.

Main Idea: Stating a Goal

When you do something, you usually have a goal in mind. You want to make something, get something, fix something, or achieve something. Reaching that goal is the main idea behind a how-to essay. When you write a how-to essay, you explain to your readers how to reach a goal.

Usually the main idea is stated in the introduction of a how-to essay. Sometimes writers also use the introduction to motivate readers to reach the goal. By describing the benefits of following the instructions, writers can make readers want to follow all the steps.

As you read the following how-to essay, ask yourself, "What goal is the writer explaining how to reach? What are the benefits of reaching the goal?"

Throw Away Your Fork

If you are not Asian, you may eat your chicken chow mein with a fork. But if you follow these steps, you can learn to eat with chopsticks. Eating with chopsticks is fun, and it makes the food taste even better!

First, hold one chopstick between your thumb and your index finger. Brace the bottom of the chopstick (the tapered, or more pointed, end) against the top of your fourth finger. Next, hold the other chopstick with your thumb, index finger, and middle finger. That is the same way you would hold a pencil. Now, place the ends of the chopsticks around a bit of food. When you squeeze the ends of the chopsticks together, you can pick up the food.

The next time you eat Chinese food, try using chopsticks. Eating with them takes a little patience, but with practice, you will get used to it. Before you know it, you will be ready to throw away your fork!

The main idea of the essay is clearly stated in the introduction. The goal is to learn how to use chopsticks. The benefit of reaching the goal is also clearly stated. According to the writer, eating with chopsticks is fun, and it makes the food taste better.

Exercise 1

Read the essay. Underline the main-idea sentence in the introduction. Then underline the sentence that states a benefit.

Strike!

Getting a strike is the aim of every bowler. To reach this goal, you must deliver the ball properly. Here are the steps that a right-handed bowler should take. If you follow them, you will improve your chance of bowling a strike.

First, face the pins, keeping your feet together. Hold the ball slightly above your waist.

Second, step forward on your right foot. As you step, extend your right arm and then step forward on your left foot. As you step, bring the ball back behind you.

Third, move your right foot forward just as the ball is as far back as your arm can go. Then slide your left foot forward. As you slide, swing the ball down and forward. Finally, stop your slide and release the ball, thumb first. Let your right hand move forward and up.

Learning these steps takes time and practice. But once you have learned them, you will be a better bowler.

Check your answers on page 186.

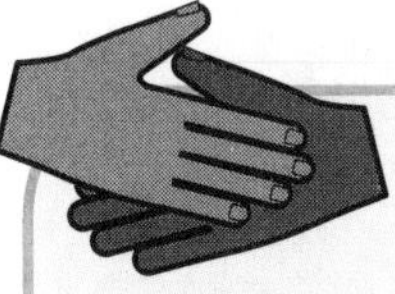

With a Partner

To get people to buy a product, advertisers show the benefits of owning the product or of using it. For example, some TV commercials hint that wearing a particular cologne will make a man more handsome and popular. Here are other benefits often used to motivate people to buy products:

- saving time or money
- feeling younger or healthier
- feeling personal satisfaction
- protecting one's family
- becoming more skilled
- enjoying oneself

With your partner, analyze some TV or magazine advertisements. Decide which benefits are suggested in each advertisement.

Developing the Main Idea: Steps in the Process

A how-to essay does more than just state a goal. It gives steps that explain how to reach the goal. Together, these steps form a **process**.

Look at the following paragraphs from the essay on bowling. Notice the underlined words. They tell each **step**—each action—that should be taken to bowl a strike.

> First, face the pins, keeping your feet together. Hold the ball slightly above your waist.
>
> Second, step forward on your right root. As you step, extend your right arm and then step forward on your left foot. As you step, bring the ball back behind you.

Do you know the part of speech of the underlined words? These words are verbs, or action words. Each verb tells the action that must be taken during a step in the process.

When you explain how to do something, it is important to include all the steps in the process. If you give incomplete instructions, your readers may not be able to reach the goal.

Be sure to explain specialized words and the tools needed to complete the process. Remember that your readers' background and experience may be different from your own. For example, if you do a lot of cooking, you probably know the specialized term *sauté*. Because you know the word, you may believe that everyone else does too. However, people who do not cook may have heard the word but not know exactly what it means. They may need to have the word explained.

When you write a how-to essay, put yourself in your readers' place. Think of ways to help your readers understand the process you are explaining.

In Your Journal

Can you cut someone's hair? Explain the best route from one place to another? Do a magic trick? Make a free throw?

Start a list of things you know how to do. The list will come in handy when you write a how-to essay.

Exercise 2

PART A

Underline the action words in each step.

To make a California sandwich, take two pieces of wheat bread. Spread one piece of bread with a teaspoon of mayonnaise. Then put a slice of Colby cheese on top of the mayonnaise. Layer lettuce, bean sprouts, and tomato on top of the cheese. Cover the sandwich with the second piece of bread,, and then cut the sandwich in half.

PART B

You need to explain to a small child how to use a cell phone. What steps should the child take? List the steps. Underline the verb in each step.

____

____

____

____

____

PART C

Each of these phrases uses specialized terms. Choose one phrase that you recognize and define it. Or define a phrase that describes a process that you use in a hobby or an activity that you do often.

- basting a hem
- bleeding the brakes
- snapping a football
- choking a guitar string
- creaming butter and sugar

Phrase: ____________________________________

Definition: __________________________________

____

Check your answers on page 186.

Organizing Ideas: Time Order

What's the best way to organize a how-to essay? Steps in a how-to essay should be organized in time order. Otherwise, readers will end up very confused. Imagine trying to follow disorganized instructions like these.

Put six chicken thighs in a well-greased baking dish. Cover and bake at 350° for 50 minutes. Before placing the dish in the oven, put a bed of rice under the chicken. You should marinate (soak) the chicken for several hours in a good teriyaki sauce. I like Johnson's, which you can find at almost any grocery store. Be sure to preheat the oven. The rice tastes better if you put a few cooked mushrooms and a little melted butter in it.

This recipe is difficult to follow because the steps are not in the right order. Here are the revised instructions.

Marinate (soak) six chicken thighs in teriyaki sauce for several hours. My favorite sauce is Johnson's, which you can find at almost any grocery store.

About an hour and a half before serving time, cook enough white rice to make three cups. Follow the instructions on the box. While the rice is cooking, melt three tablespoons of butter over low heat. Add a half cup of sliced mushrooms and cook until tender. When the rice is ready, stir in the mushrooms and butter.

Next, put the rice mixture in the bottom of a well-greased baking dish. Spread the rice around evenly so it forms a bed. Then, put the marinated thighs on top of the rice.

Finally, cover the chicken and bake it at 350° for 50 minutes or until done.

The revised instructions are easier to follow because the steps are more clearly organized (and more fully explained). Notice that the steps in the new instructions are introduced by transitions. Words such as *then*, *while*, and *next* link one step to the next. The transitions help readers keep track of what must be done and when it must be done. Be sure to use time-order transitions to link the steps in your how-to essays.

Time-Order Transitions

first	now	when	while
second	then	after	next
third	meanwhile	before	finally

Exercise 3

Put the steps below in time order. Number the first step 1, the second step 2, and so on. Then use the steps to write a paragraph. Be sure to link the steps with time-order transitions.

Topic: Going grocery shopping

_________ Get a shopping cart.

_________ Make a grocery list.

_________ Go to the store.

_________ Pay the cashier.

_________ Empty your cart at the checkout.

_________ Go up and down the aisles, selecting food.

_________ Take your food home.

Paragraph: ____

____

____

____

____

____

____

____

____

Check your answers on page 186.

Read a How-To Essay

You have studied three elements of how-to essays: the main idea (or goal to be reached), the steps necessary for reaching the goal, and the order to put the steps in. Look for these elements as you read the following essays.

Have you ever thought about doing home improvements but did not know where to begin? This essay can help you get started.

How to Arrange a Room

(1) Think about your favorite room in your home. What do you like about it? Is there a way you could improve the room without spending a great deal of time or money? Now think about your least favorite room. What do you dislike about it? How could you improve that room?

(2) The best low-cost way to improve any room is to rearrange the furniture. Rearranging a room, however, is not as simple as it sounds. Moving furniture may make the room look worse. Arranging a room so it satisfies your needs and pleases your eye takes some effort. Follow these steps to improve a room in your home.

(3) First, get a sense of your own style. Look at design magazines, store displays, and friends' homes. Do you prefer a room packed with furniture and knickknacks or a room that has only a few pieces of furniture? Does a mixture of styles make you feel uneasy, or do you like variety? Later in this process, you may discover that you need to add or remove some pieces of furniture. Knowing what you like will help you make decisions about the changes you want to make.

(4) Next, decide what role—or roles—your room needs to fulfill. A living room, for example, needs to provide seating so people can talk with one another. Many rooms have more than one purpose. A bedroom, for example, may also serve as an office. Think about the activities that take place in your room at various times.

(5) Third, evaluate the furniture currently in the room. Does each piece have a purpose? Or are some pieces there simply because they do not fit anywhere else in your home? Decide whether removing some furniture could improve the room's usefulness. For example, your dining room may also serve as a study for your children. Does the extra TV really belong in the dining room?

(6) Consider, too, whether more furniture is needed. The dining room/study may need a bookcase or cupboard so the children's books and supplies are not scattered in several rooms. If your bedroom is also your office, replacing a card table with a small desk that has drawers might be a good idea.

(7) Next, plan your new room arrangement. For this step, you will need a tape measure and some graph paper. Measure the room. Then draw the walls on a sheet of graph paper. Let each square equal one square foot. On the wall lines, mark the doors and windows. Next, measure each piece of furniture. Using more graph paper, draw each piece, label it, and cut it out. Make additional templates for furniture that you might want to add to the room. Then lay out your furniture templates on the room grid. Try various arrangements until you come up with one that pleases you.

LANGUAGE Tip

Be an active reader. Underline or highlight important points. Place a question mark in the margin when you do not understand an idea. Then you can ask someone for help later.

(8) Here are a few guidelines for your plan:

(a) If the room has more than one purpose, group the furniture according to those purposes. For example, if a room is both a family room and a dining room, keep the china cabinet near the dining table and the TV near the couch.

(b) For easy movement around the room, leave at least three feet of space around each furniture grouping. Make sure that doors, windows, and pathways through the room are not blocked.

(c) Provide for both variety and balance. For example, don't put all the tall pieces together on one side of the room. Instead, make the room more interesting by alternating pieces of different heights.

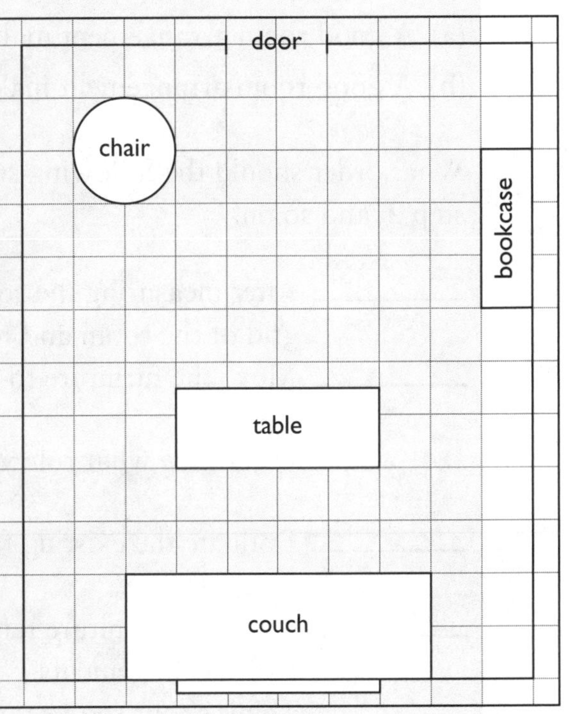

(9) If you find that your room is too crowded, think about what furniture you could get rid of. Or, if you have more space than you expected, consider what piece of furniture you could add, how big it should be, and what it should look like.

(10) Finally, when you are satisfied with your plan, move the furniture. Look carefully at your new arrangement. If you do not like the way the room looks, go back to the planning stage. If you are satisfied with the new arrangement, use the room for a few days. You may find that some small changes will make your room just perfect.

Check Your Understanding

Answer each question about "How to Arrange a Room." Look back at the essay if you need to.

1. What is the main idea in "How to Arrange a Room"? Circle the correct letter.
   (a) Different people have different ideas of what makes a good room arrangement.
   (b) By following certain steps, the appearance and usefulness of almost any room can be improved.

2. According to the author, what is the benefit of rearranging the furniture in a room? Circle the correct letter.
   (a) A good room arrangement makes the room more pleasant and easier to use.
   (b) A good room arrangement makes the room easier to clean.

3. What order should the following steps be in? Number the first step 1, the second step 2, and so on.

   ________ After measuring the room and the furniture, use graph paper to make a grid of the room and templates of the furniture.
   ________ Move the furniture to match your plan.

   ________ Determine what role your room has.

   ________ Evaluate the existing furniture in the room and decide whether all of it is useful.
   ________ Move the furniture templates about on the graph paper grid in various room arrangements.
   ________ Think about rooms you enjoy being in or looking at.

4. In this essay, what does the word *template* (paragraph 7) mean? Circle the correct letter.
   (a) a model of a real thing
   (b) a pattern that can be used to make something

5. List four time-order transitions that are used in the essay.

   (a) ____________________ (b) ____________________

   (c) ____________________ (d) ____________________

Check your answers on page 186.

Write a How-To Essay

Prewriting: Selecting a Topic and a Purpose

"How to Arrange a Room" gives step-by-step instructions for improving the space you live in. **Write a how-to essay in which you give step-by-step instructions.** Your purpose is to describe. The topic you choose to describe could be

- a life skill
- a sport or athletic skill
- a job skill
- a skill used in a hobby

Below are some ideas to get you started. Choose *one* of these topics or use a topic of your own. Check your journal for ideas. You may have written about something you do well that you would enjoy explaining in an essay.

- how to start a car
- how to paint a wall
- how to cook a dinner
- how to lift weights
- how to cut your child's hair
- how to give a baby a bath
- how to change a diaper
- how to put on makeup

Write your topic here.

Topic: ____

Prewriting: Developing Your Topic

Now that you have your topic, you need to think of details so you can develop the topic. Think of the steps in the process you're going to explain. Picture the process in your mind. Imagine yourself going slowly through each step. As you think, freewrite. (You learned about freewriting in Chapter 2.) To freewrite, put your pencil or pen on the paper and keep writing. As you imagine the process, write down everything you see in your mind.

Here is one student's freewriting about how to do a sit-up.

I am lying on my back with my hands clasped behind my head and my knees bent. My feet are on the floor. My elbows are bent and are resting on the floor too. Slowly I pull my tummy muscles in while I push down my lower back. My shoulders and head raise off the ground. I am breathing out at this point. I hold myself up for a little bit and then come back down, breathing out. Oh, yeah—all this time my head is tilted back and my eyes are looking toward the ceiling.

Picture yourself doing the skill you want to explain. On the lines below, freewrite about all the steps you see yourself going through.

Prewriting: Organizing Your Ideas

Finish prewriting by organizing your ideas.

Write a main-idea sentence.

Ask yourself, "What goal do I want my readers to reach?"

Main-idea sentence: ______________________________

____

____

____

Group the steps in your process.

Decide whether you need one, two, or more paragraphs for the body of your essay. Draw a line around the steps that go together. Or, if you prefer, draw clusters showing how the steps go together.

Decide what order to put your steps in.

Number your steps in the order you want them in. Follow the student's example.

② I'm lying on my back with my hands clasped behind my head and my knees bent. ①My feet are on the floor. ③My elbows are bent and are resting on the floor too. ① Slowly I pull my tummy muscles in while I push down my lower back. ② My shoulders and head raise off the ground. ③ I'm breathing out at this point. ⑤I hold myself up for a little bit and then come back down, breathing out. ④ Oh, yeah—all this time my head is tilted back and my eyes are looking toward the ceiling.

Drafting

The next stage of the writing process is drafting. During this stage, you use your prewriting plan to write a first draft. Remember that a first draft is just a first try. You'll have a chance to improve your writing when you revise and edit.

Using your prewriting plan, write a first draft on the topic of your choice. If you need more space, continue writing on a piece of paper.

State a goal in the introduction.

Use transitions to link steps.

End with a restatement of the goal.

Revising

The next stage is to evaluate your first draft. You may do this alone or with a partner. First, do the Revision Warm-Up. Then use the Revision Checklist to revise your draft.

Revision Warm-Up

Follow the directions below.

1. Find one step that is out of order. Draw an arrow to show where that step belongs.
2. Add these two steps where they belong.
   - As you rise, breathe out.
   - As you lower your body, breathe in.

Sit Up!

Exercise is important. Avoiding injury is just as important. Sit-ups can keep you fit, but you must be careful to do them properly.

It is important to start out in the correct position. Keep your feet on the floor, about shoulder distance apart. Lie on your back with your knees up and bent. Clasp your hands and rest them on the back of your neck.

Now pull in your lower "tummy" muscles. At the same time, push your lower back into the floor. Your head and shoulders should naturally rise from the floor. Be sure to keep your head and elbows back and look toward the ceiling. Hold this position. Then relax and lower your upper body.

If you follow these steps, you will do sit-ups correctly. Soon you will have a firmer and more attractive tummy.

Check your answers on page 186.

☑ Revision Checklist

Yes	No	
❑	❑	1. Does the introductory paragraph state a goal?
❑	❑	2. Does the introduction state the benefit of learning the process?
❑	❑	3. Does the body include all the steps in the process?
❑	❑	4. Are all the steps in the process clear?
❑	❑	5. Are the steps in time order?
❑	❑	6. Are the steps linked by time-order transitions?
❑	❑	7. Does the essay have a concluding paragraph?

Editing

The last stage of the writing process is editing. During this stage, you look for and correct errors in grammar, mechanics, and usage.

Do the Editing Exercise. Then edit the draft of your essay. Look for and correct noun, pronoun, and verb errors as well as other errors. If possible, work with a partner.

Editing Exercise: Verbs

Underline and correct the verb error in each sentence.

Two Different People

My ex-girlfriend and I seen eye to eye on very few things. One of the many things we could not agreed on was movies. She liked action movies—the kind in which the bad guys are kill off by a hero. She was not happy unless a car or two and maybe a building were blew up. I have always hate violent movies. I like well-wrote, upbeat stories about people overcoming their problems.

One Saturday night, our differences come to a head. We have just finished dinner and were arguing about what movie to see. She has been wanting to see an Arnold Schwarzenegger movie, but I wanted to see a movie about baseball. As we argued, each of us grown more stubborn.

Finally, we done the only thing we could do. We gone to the same theater but not to the same movie. That very evening, we breaked off our relationship. We haven't spoke to each other since then. I should have knew better than to date someone whose taste was so different from mine.

Check your answers on page 186–187.

Giving Examples

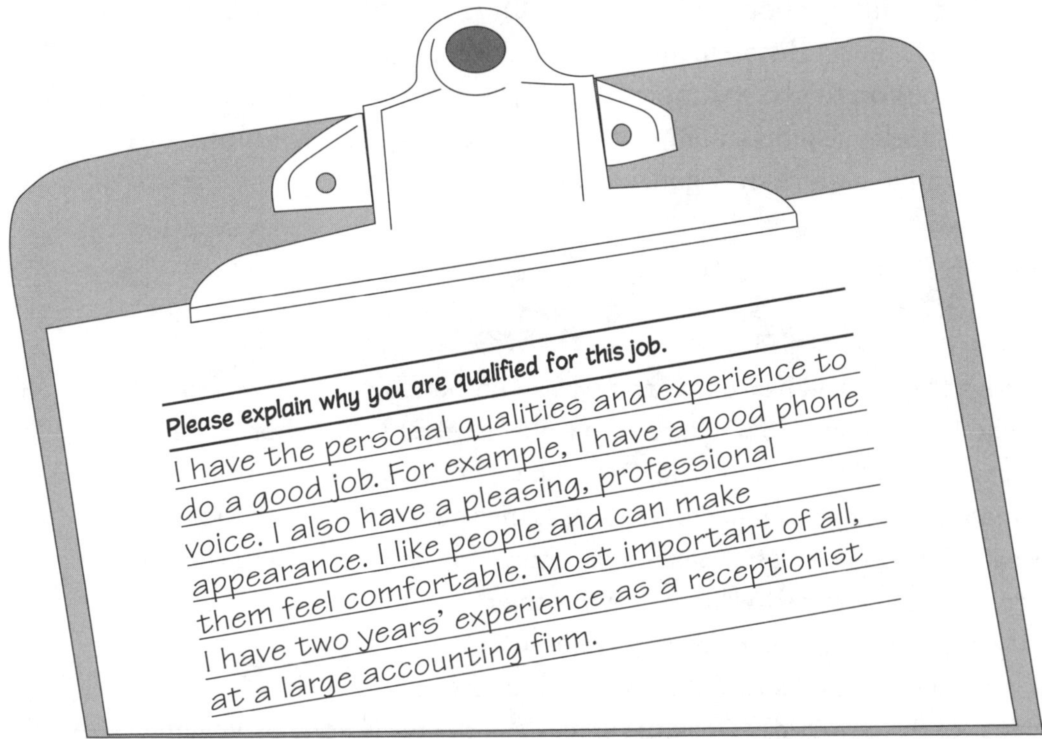

Please explain why you are qualified for this job.
I have the personal qualities and experience to
do a good job. For example, I have a good phone
voice. I also have a pleasing, professional
appearance. I like people and can make
them feel comfortable. Most important of all,
I have two years' experience as a receptionist
at a large accounting firm.

Is the person who wrote this paragraph qualified for the job? She says she is. Then she gives examples of what makes her qualified. Since the examples are well chosen, you are likely to agree with her. Giving examples is a common way of explaining. In this chapter, you will learn how to use examples to explain and support a main idea.

After working through this chapter, you should be able to

- find the main idea of an essay that gives examples
- identify supporting examples
- organize examples in order of importance
- prewrite, draft, revise, and edit an essay of example

Elements of Essays of Example

This section answers three basic questions about the essay of example: How is the essay organized? Why use examples? What order should the examples be in?

Main Idea: General Statement

An essay of example often starts with a general statement. The statement could be about the world. It could be about life or people. Or it could be about the writer himself or herself. The general statement is the essay's main idea.

The essay then goes on to give examples that support the statement. The point of the essay is to show why the general statement is true. The essay below follows this statement-and-example pattern of organization.

Who Cares?

Before I moved here, I had heard that this was an unfriendly town. It was said that the people who live here just do not care about one another. In the short time I have lived here, I have learned that is not true. People here are always willing to help out.

When someone is facing huge medical expenses, neighbors often raise money to pay for the bills. For example, last weekend my church group ran a special car wash. We collected $500 to help the Wilkinses pay for their child's operation. The Elks club is also holding a fund-raising dinner for the Wilkinses.

Another example of people's caring attitude is the town's new shelter for the homeless. Most of the day-to-day work of running the shelter is done by volunteers. They greet people at the door and answer the phones. They discuss job leads with clients and serve them hot coffee. They also hand out blankets and bedrolls and do several other chores.

The literacy program at our public library is yet another example of people's caring attitude. Many townspeople support the program by acting as volunteer tutors. They give up their free time to help other adults learn to read and write. Volunteers also run an after-school tutoring program. Children can go there for help with their homework.

These are just a few of the townspeople's acts of kindness. Although I have not been here long, I have seen many such acts. I am proud to say that the people in this town truly care about one another.

The main idea is that townspeople are always willing to help one another. Each paragraph in the body gives an example to support this general statement.

Exercise 1

Read the essay. Then underline the main idea in the introduction.

Too Much Violence

Our kids see too much violence on TV. I realized this about my own children just last Saturday.

That morning my three kids were watching cartoons. Every time I glanced at the TV, one cartoon character was kicking or hitting or shooting another character.

That afternoon the kids watched an old *Three Stooges* movie. The children giggled when Moe pulled out Larry's hair. They howled with laughter when Moe poked Curly in the eye. I was not amused—especially when the kids began imitating what they saw.

Unfortunately the worst violence the kids saw last Saturday was on the evening news. Story after story told about a real person being hurt or killed by someone else. Is it really necessary to report on every violent crime?

Viewing all that violence must have a bad effect on children. Kids grow up too fast today. Parents don't need TV speeding up the process.

Check your answers on page 187.

In Your Journal

Your journal is an excellent place to write comments. As you observe the world, write about what you see and think about. When you make a comment, note one or two examples that will help you remember what you saw or what you were thinking about.

Here are some general statements to help you get started. Choose one or two. Add examples to support the comment.

- TV is filled with annoying commercials.
- This year's fashions are crazier than ever.
- There are a lot of bad drivers on the road.
- Hard times can bring out the best in people.

Developing the Main Idea: Examples

You have seen how examples can be used to support a general statement. But what is an example? An **example** is a specific situation or instance. The general statement, or main idea, is "big." It might refer to many people, places, or things. In contrast, an example is "small." It might refer to only one person, place, or thing. Look again at the essay on page 80. Think about the relationship between the general statement ("People here are always willing to help out") and the examples that support that statement.

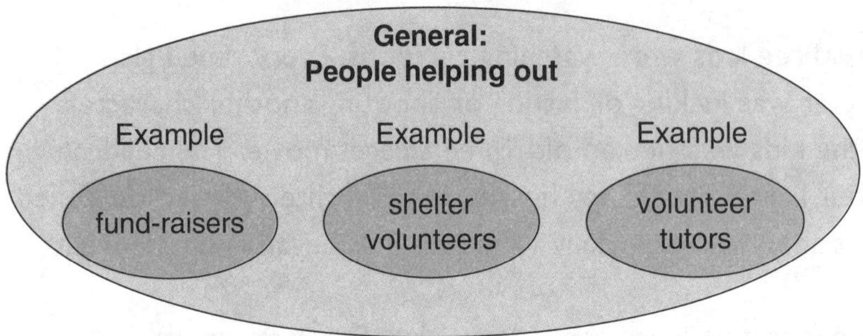

The bigger circle stands for the general statement. This circle includes everyone in the community. The smaller circles stand for the examples. Each small circle refers to a small group of people within the community.

Examples are used in all kinds of writing. Examples are especially important in writing that explains. That is because examples show what a writer means.

Imagine reading an essay and finding this general statement: "You should devote yourself to things that really matter." To you, "things that really matter" might be earning money and building a career. To another reader, "things that really matter" might be home and family. Other readers may have still other meanings for the general statement. Did the writer mean all of these ideas—or none of them? Examples would clear up the mystery.

When you make a general statement, do not leave your readers wondering what you mean. Back up the "big" with the "small." Explain by giving examples.

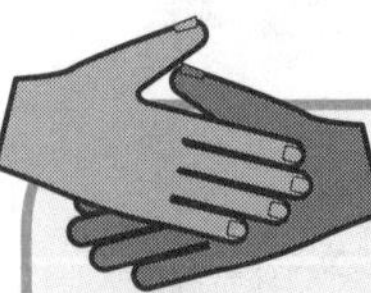

With a Partner

Together, choose one or two of the general ideas below. In your journal write examples that show what the idea means to you. Do not talk over the examples or show them to your partner. When you're both finished, compare notes. Did the ideas mean exactly the same thing to both of you?

- a good job
- a delicious meal
- a great time
- the best music

Exercise 2

Listed below are the examples and the main ideas for three essays. Match the examples and the main ideas. Write the examples on the lines below each main idea.

Examples

- There is the deep and vast Grand Canyon.
- Salsa now outsells ketchup.
- Store clerks are impatient when they cannot understand you.
- You cannot understand what people are saying on TV shows.
- There are the high snowcapped Rocky Mountains.
- There is the huge, watery Everglades swamp.
- There are more than 50 Mexican restaurants in the city.
- You cannot ask for directions.
- Tortilla chips and salsa seem to be served at every party.

Main Ideas

1. Mexican food is becoming more and more popular.

____

____

____

2. There is a national park for you, no matter what kind of landscape you like.

____

____

____

3. Living in a country where you do not speak the language is difficult.

____

____

____

Check your answer on page 187.

Organizing Ideas: Order of Importance

Sometimes all the examples in an essay are equally important. Each example carries the same weight in supporting the main idea. Look again at the essay "Who Cares?" on page 80. Each example in the essay is just as important as the others.

Main Idea	→	The townspeople are willing to help one another.
Example 1	→	One important example: fund-raisers
Example 2	→	One important example: shelter volunteers
Example 3	→	One important example: volunteer tutors

In other essays, one or two examples may be more important than the other examples. To show which examples carry the most weight, writers may put the examples in **order of importance**—usually from least important to most important. Look again at the job application at the beginning of this chapter. It is organized in order of importance.

Main Idea	→	I have the qualities and experience to do a good job.
Example 1	→	Least important example: good phone voice
Example 2	→	More important example: pleasing appearance
Example 3	→	More important example: like people
Example 4	→	Most important example: two years' experience

The writer ends with her strongest note. Concluding with the best example helps build a strong case.

Notice the transition that the writer uses before the last example. She begins the sentence with the words *most important of all.* There are other transitions that show **order of importance.** If you are giving examples of good times in your life, the transition could be "The best time in my life was . . ." If you are giving examples of bad times, you might write, "The worst time in my life was . . ."

When you place examples in order of importance, use a transition showing that the most important, the most dramatic, or the most extreme example is coming last.

Order-of-Importance Transitions

little—less—least	good—better—best
much—more—most	bad—worse—worst

Exercise 3

Read the essay. Then circle the letter describing the order of examples used in the essay.

An Annoying Coworker

I like almost everyone I work with. However, there is one coworker who really annoys me. His name is Barry, and he has some very bad habits.

One of his habits is borrowing items without asking. Whenever I am not around, he takes my pen or my glue or my scissors. Then when I reach for my supplies, they are not there.

Worse yet, Barry makes a lot of personal phone calls. He does not lower his voice when he is on the phone. Focusing on my work is hard when Barry is yak-yak-yakking with his girlfriend.

Perhaps Barry's worst habit is butting into other people's conversations. On three occasions, he has interrupted me while I was talking with a client. Each time I was answering a question. Each time Barry said I was giving the wrong answer. (But I wasn't!) It was very embarrassing.

I have talked to Barry about his annoying habits. Every time he has said that he was sorry and that he would change. He has not changed yet, and I doubt that he ever will.

(a) equal importance
(b) order of importance

Check your answers on page 187.

Read an Essay of Example

You have studied three elements of an essay of example: the general-statement main idea, examples, and ways to organize examples. Look for these elements as you read the following essay.

This writer uses the Internet for many purposes. Notice the many examples listed. Each example would help someone who does not use the Internet understand why the Internet is an important tool in the modern world.

A Web of Possibilities

(1) Imagine life without the Internet. If you are like most people today, you would feel lost if the Internet suddenly disappeared. We have come to rely on it in many ways.

(2) Do you want to go to a movie or a concert? Check the Internet for a list of show times and prices. Do you want to go out to dinner? Online, you can find lists of local restaurants. In addition, you can read reviews of the restaurants. These reviews are written by customers who are not afraid to give their honest opinions. The same is true for hotels, motels, and tourist attractions.

(3) Quite often you do not have time for shopping at a local store. The Internet comes in handy. You can purchase whatever you need online. The variety of products available on the Internet is amazing. Everything from baby bibs to car parts is for sale online. In addition, online prices are often lower than the prices at your local stores.

(4) Suppose you are looking for a new apartment. Why not start your search on the Web? Many sites list apartments for rent. You can even download a rental application and submit it online. If you are in the market for a new home, why waste time driving from one house to the next? First spend a few hours searching through real estate Web sites. In that way, you narrow down your search to a few houses that are worth a visit.

(5) Web sites can supply just about any information. Are you looking for the population of India? Do you want to know the date when Elvis Presley was born? It is all on the Web. Online dictionaries define words, and some even pronounce the words for you. If you have a question about your health, you might want to check a medical Web site before seeing your doctor.

(6) Do you need to know how to get to the doctor's office (or anywhere else, for that matter)? Online sites can give you driving directions to almost anywhere in the country. They will tell you which direction to turn and provide a map you can take along on your trip. Some Web sites even show you where you are likely to run into delays on your route.

(7) Online financial Web sites provide a number of important services. You can use them to apply for home mortgages or other loans. You can sign up for a savings account, CD, or a checking account. Some sites let you pay your bills online.

(8) Not too many years ago, most people subscribed to a daily newspaper. Today, often without charge, news Web sites offer breaking news from around the world. Now you can read about events as they happen. You do not have to wait for the story in the next day's edition. Weather Web sites keep you informed about dangerous storms headed your way. Some show radar maps so you can track the weather fronts yourself.

(9) Of course, one important reason to use the Internet is to communicate. With electronic mail (e-mail), you write messages when you have time. Then when your friends have time, they can read your messages. At work, you can leave messages for your fellow workers throughout the day. You do not have to wait for people to be free before talking to them. If you want immediate feedback, you can take part in a chat room. Chat rooms allow you to type in messages to people around the world who are online at the same time.

(10) When we want to be entertained, shop, or find a new home, we use the Internet. When we want to look up facts or keep up on the news, we use the Internet. When we want to communicate, we use the Internet. The Internet has become part of our daily lives. Every day we are more amazed at its possibilities, and we become more dependent on it. Life without the Internet has become unthinkable.

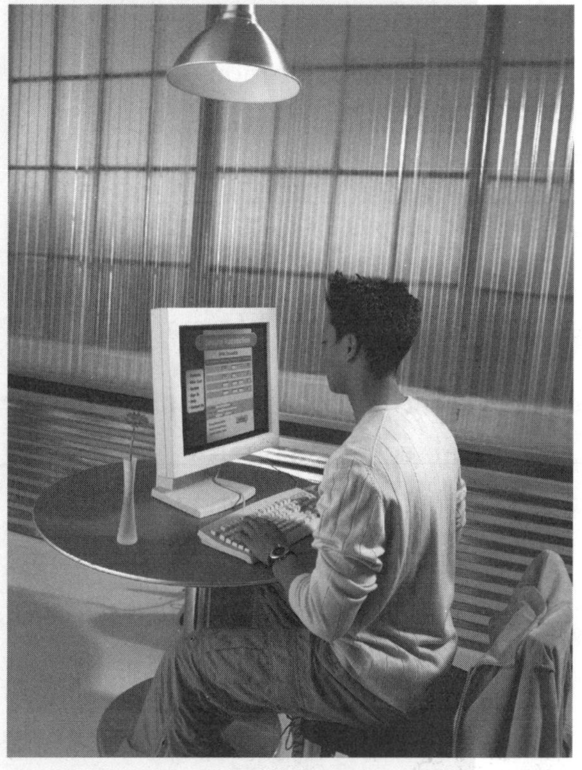

LANGUAGE Tip

The address of an Internet site tells who has put this information on the Web.

.com comes from a business
.edu comes from a school
.gov comes from a government office
.org comes from a non-profit organization

Check Your Understanding

PART A

Answer each question about "A Web of Possibilities." Look back at the essay if you need to.

1. What is the main idea of "A Web of Possibilities"? Circle the letter of the correct answer.
   (a) People should be concerned that they may become addicted to the Internet.
   (b) The Internet has become very important to many people.

2. Tell in which paragraph each example appears.

(a) entertainment information	paragraph ____
(b) facts and definitions	paragraph ____
(c) communication	paragraph ____
(d) financial services	paragraph ____
(e) shopping options	paragraph ____
(f) news	paragraph ____
(g) travel directions	paragraph ____
(h) real estate information	paragraph ____

3. Which order did the author put the examples in? Circle the correct letter.
   (a) equal importance
   (b) order of importance

PART B

Answer each question in a sentence or two.

1. What other examples could the author have used to explain the main idea? Write one example based on your own experience.

   ____

   ____

2. Where in the conclusion does the author restate the main idea? Copy the sentence.

   ____

   ____

Check your answers on page 187.

Write an Essay of Example

Prewriting: Selecting a Topic and a Purpose

In "A Web of Possibilities," the author makes a general statement about the usefulness of the Internet. Then she lists examples to show what she means. **Write your own essay about something that is happening in the world today.**

Look around you, and make a comment about the people and the events that you see. Include examples to show what you mean. Your purpose is to explain. The topic you choose to describe could be

- everyday living
- sports
- fashion
- politics

Below are some ideas to get you started. Choose *one* of these topics or use a topic of your own. Check your journal for ideas. You may have made a general comment that you would enjoy explaining in an essay. Don't forget to use descriptive details to help your readers picture your examples.

- ways that everyday life is easier than in the past
- people acting rudely
- ways you enjoy spending your free time
- today's great athletes
- clothes that have come back into style
- ways the government works (or does not work) for us

Write your topic here.

Topic: ____

Prewriting: Developing Your Topic

Now that you have your topic, you need to think of examples so you can develop the topic. Brainstorming is a good way to get ideas for an essay of example. (You learned about brainstorming in Chapter 2.)

Here are the notes that a student made while brainstorming. His topic was bad drivers.

1. Don't see stop signs
2. Busy talking on cell phone, don't notice light has changed
3. Forget to use turn signals
4. Speed on side streets
5. Don't care if kids get hurt
6. Tailgate all the time

On the lines below, list examples to develop your topic. Follow the student's example and use brainstorming. Or, if you prefer, use a different method, such as questioning or freewriting.

Prewriting: Organizing Your Ideas

Finish prewriting by organizing your ideas.

Write a main-idea sentence.

Your main idea is the general statement you want to make. If you are not sure what your general statement is, ask yourself, "What are all my examples about?"

Main-idea sentence: ____

____

____

Group your supporting examples.

Decide whether you need one, two, or more paragraphs for the body of your essay. Draw a line around the examples that go together. Or, if you prefer, draw clusters showing how the examples go together. Follow the student's example.

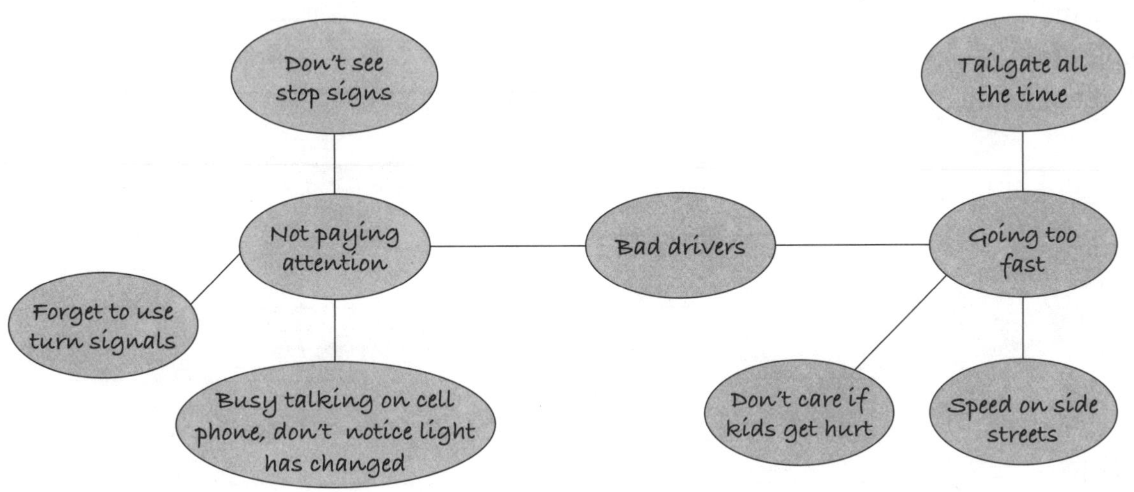

Decide what order to put your supporting examples in.

Are some of your examples more important than others? Or are all your examples of equal importance? Number your examples so you can put them in order. **Describe how you ordered your examples here.**

Order: ____

____

Drafting

The next stage of the writing process is drafting. During this stage, you use your prewriting plan to write a first draft. Remember that a first draft is just a first try. You will have a chance to improve your writing when you revise and edit.

Using your prewriting plan, write a first draft on the topic of your choice. If you need more space, continue writing on a piece of paper.

Include a main-idea sentence in the introduction.

Use specific examples to develop the main idea.

End with a restatement of the main idea.

Revising

The next stage is to evaluate your first draft. You may do this alone or with a partner. First, do the Revision Warm-Up. Then use the Revision Checklist to revise your draft.

Revision Warm-Up

Follow the directions below.

1. Add a transition to the beginning of paragraph 3 to show that the most important examples are coming up.
2. Add a concluding paragraph that includes a restatement of the main idea.

Bad Drivers

Every time I drive, I cannot help noticing that drivers are getting worse and worse. I am surprised that the accident rate is not higher than it is.

Too many people just don't pay attention to their driving. When they make a turn, they forget to use their turn signals. They are so busy changing the station on the radio or talking on their cell phones that they don't seem to notice the light has changed. They also run stop signs too often.

Many people drive much too fast. I see tailgaters every time I drive on the highway. They are in such a hurry that they don't keep a safe distance from the other drivers. Speeding drivers have also made the side streets dangerous. The street I live on used to be quiet, but speeding cars have made it unsafe. The speeders just don't care about the kids playing near the street. Will it take a tragedy to make these drivers slow down?

____

____

Check your answers on pages 187–188.

Revision Checklist

Yes	No	
❑	❑	1. Is there a main-idea sentence in the introduction?
❑	❑	2. Is the body well developed with examples?
❑	❑	3. Do all the examples explain, or support, the main idea?
❑	❑	4. Are the examples logically organized?
❑	❑	5. Does the conclusion restate the main idea?
❑	❑	6. Are all the sentences and ideas clear?

Editing

The last stage of the writing process is editing. During this stage, you look for and correct errors in grammar, mechanics, and usage.

Do the Editing Exercise. Then edit the draft of your essay. Look for and correct noun, pronoun, verb, and adjective and adverb errors. Also look for other kinds of errors. If possible, work with a partner.

Editing Exercise: Adjectives and Adverbs

Underline and correct the adjective or adverb error in each sentence.

Picky Pet

My cat, Murphy, is the most pickiest eater in the world. I have given her every brand of cat food on the market, but she does not like none of them. Each time I give her a new brand, she acts as if it is the worse food she has ever eaten. Yesterday I finally decided to do something to make her less fussier. I decided I would not give her nothing to eat until she had cleaned up her plate.

Last night she began to meow pitiful. She had not touched the food I had given her, and the food looked terribly. It had been sitting so long that it was complete dry. She continued to meow sad, but I pretended to ignore her.

Suddenly I heard a loudly noise in the kitchen. I quick ran to see what had happened. Murphy had flipped her bowl over and was making the worstest mess I had ever seen. The cat meowed loud and happily as I opened a can of tuna. I hated to give in, but I figured it was more better than putting up with her tantrums.

Check your answers on page 188.

Chapter 7

Test Skill

Comparing and Contrasting

Candidates for Representative

	Grassroots Party **CISNEROS**	*Citizens' Party* **MARKS**

Taxes	Supports a raise	Supports a freeze
Gun Control	Favors waiting period on all gun purchases	Favors waiting period on all gun purchases
Health Care	Use increased taxes for universal health care system	Increase competition in insurance markets to drive down costs
Casino Gambling	Against proposed casino complex	Supports proposed casino complex

Which of the two candidates would you vote for? To decide, you might compare and contrast each candidate's views with your own views. Comparing and contrasting are useful thinking skills. In this chapter, you will learn how to write essays that compare and contrast.

After working through this chapter, you should be able to

- identify reasons for comparing and contrasting
- show comparisons and contrasts in chart form
- organize a comparison-and-contrast essay
- prewrite, draft, revise, and edit an essay that compares and contrasts

Elements of Comparison-and-Contrast Essays

This section looks at the why, what, and how of comparison-and-contrast essays. You will learn why writers compare and contrast, what bases of comparison they use, and how they organize comparison-and-contrast essays.

Main Idea: Why Compare and Contrast?

Writers often use comparison-and-contrast essays to make a point. They want to show that one person or one thing is better than another person or thing. Read this comparison-and-contrast essay. The writer's point, or main idea, is to explain why Stephen Marks would make a better representative than Stella Cisneros.

Mark Your Ballot for Marks

You should look closely at the views of Stephen Marks and Stella Cisneros. If you study what they think about the issues, you will vote for Marks.

Both Marks and Cisneros have promised to support a two-week waiting period on gun purchases. The candidates agree on the issue of gun control, but that is where their similarities end.

Marks wants to hold the line on taxes. In fact, if elected, he would support a two-year tax freeze. In contrast, Cisneros would raise our taxes. She simply does not appreciate how hard we taxpayers work for our money.

Marks and Cisneros differ on another important issue—health care. Marks supports using competition and independence. He wants individuals to decide what is best for them. Not the government. Cisneros, on the other hand, wants the government to take over our health care.

A final difference between the candidates is their stands on the proposed downtown casino complex. Marks supports it because it will bring jobs and tax dollars. Predictably, Cisneros is against the complex.

The choice is clear. Vote for low taxes, quality independent health care, and jobs. Mark your ballot for Marks.

Not all comparison-and-contrast essays are written to convince readers that one person or thing is better than another. Sometimes writers compare and contrast just to point out similarities and differences. For example, a writer might compare and contrast her twin brothers to make the point that they look alike but their personalities differ. Another writer might compare and contrast a favorite place during summer and winter to show how one place changes over time.

Exercise 1

Read each essay. Then circle the letter of the main idea.

East and West

New York and Los Angeles are the two largest U.S. cities. Yet the two cities could not possibly be more different.

New York is a tall, dense city. Much of its land lies on islands and peninsulas. The city's skyscrapers rise to the clouds. Many New Yorkers live in large apartment buildings. Millions of people ride buses and trains to work.

On the other hand, Los Angeles is a big, low city. It stretches over miles. Its people live in valleys and canyons, on foothills and mountains. Many drive long distances to work, often on crowded highways.

(a) New York is a better place to live than Los Angeles.

(b) New York and Los Angeles are quite different.

Railway or Highway?

The price of gas is going up. As a result, travelers are turning to cheaper modes of travel. The old reliables—the bus and the train—are back in demand. Of the two, the bus is the better bargain.

Both the train and the bus can be relaxing. Both offer scenic views of the countryside. Both serve most major cities. But bus fare is usually lower than train fare. I compared train and bus fares from Chicago to three cities—New York, Dallas, and Los Angeles. In each case, the bus fare was at least 10 percent less than the train fare.

In general, the train is faster and more comfortable. But if cost really matters to you, you should take the bus.

(a) Bus travel is a better bargain than train travel.

(b) Buses and trains have their good points and bad points.

Check your answers on page 188.

Developing the Main Idea: Bases of Comparison

How do writers make comparisons and contrasts? They look for similarities and differences in the people or things they are writing about. The qualities they compare and contrast are called **bases of comparison.**

Look again at the poster at the beginning of this chapter. It contains four bases of comparison—taxes, gun control, health care, and casino gambling. Comparing and contrasting the candidates' views on those issues helps the writer show that Marks is the better candidate.

When you decide what bases to use, consider your topic and main idea. Like the writer of the political essay, choose bases that help support your main idea.

For example, suppose you want to show that one fast-food burger is better than another. What bases of comparison might you choose? You would probably want to talk about cost, taste, and fat content. These qualities would matter to most diners who were deciding which burger to buy. A chart can help you keep track of your bases of comparison.

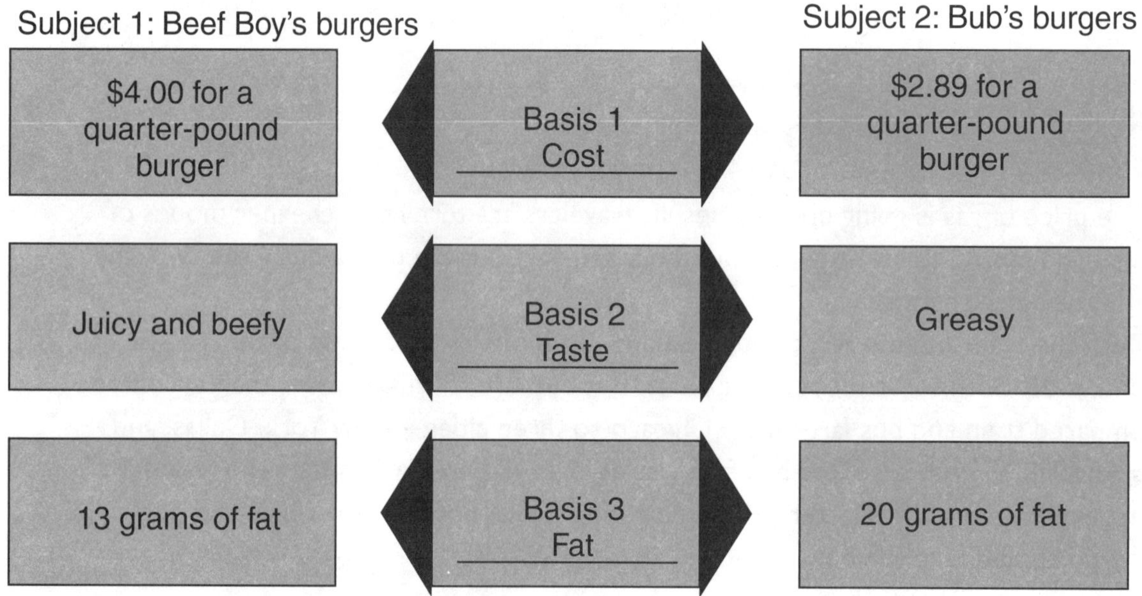

Compare and contrast two brands of a similar product, such as shampoo. Decide which qualities to discuss. Chart your bases of comparison.

Exercise 2

Read the essay. Then complete the comparison-and-contrast chart.

Day and Night

Have you ever heard the saying "Opposites attract"? This saying describes the relationship between my husband (a morning person) and me (a night person).

Even on weekends, Leon wakes up at 6:00 a.m. He jumps out of bed with a smile, ready to face the day. Meanwhile, I am curled up in my blanket, tired and grumpy. The only thing that makes me smile is the thought of going back to sleep.

If you would check in with us in the afternoon, you would see the tide turning. After doing chores all morning, Leon is beginning to feel tired. In contrast, I feel completely energized. Guess who is smiling now?

By evening, my husband's energy level is very low. When we go to a movie, there is only a 50–50 chance he will stay awake until the end of the film. I, on the other hand, am ready to go out after the movie.

As you can see, my husband and I are on completely different schedules. He gets up with the roosters, and I fly with the night owls.

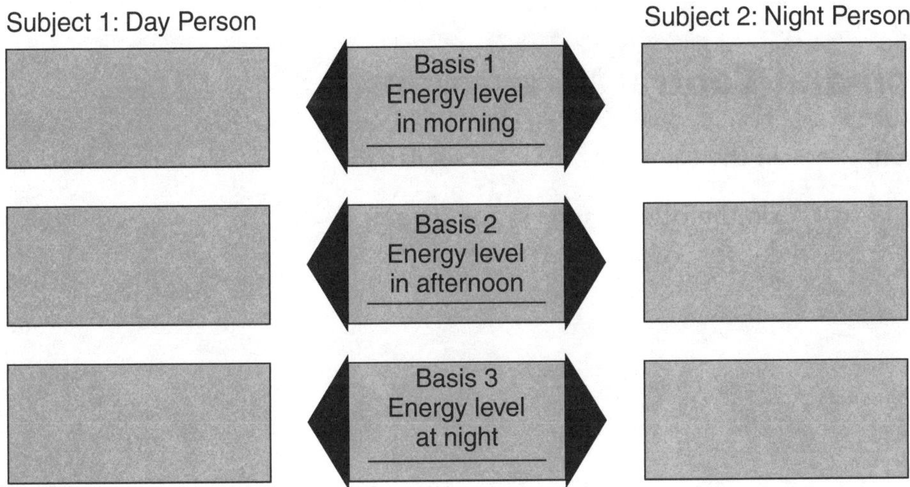

Check your answers on page 188.

Organizing Ideas: Block Pattern and Alternating Pattern

When an essay is well-organized, the reader has an easier time understanding the main point. Two good ways to organize comparison-and-contrast essays are the block pattern and the alternating pattern.

When using the block pattern, the writer discusses the first person or thing that is being compared and contrasted. Then the writer discusses the second person or thing.

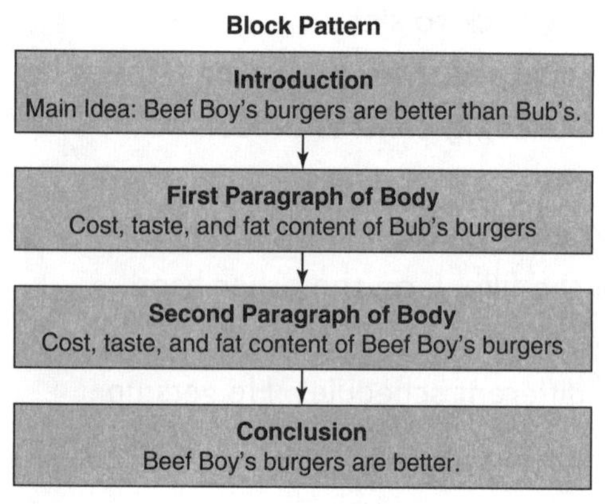

When using the alternating pattern, the writer discusses the first basis of comparison. Then, one by one, the writer discusses the other bases of comparison.

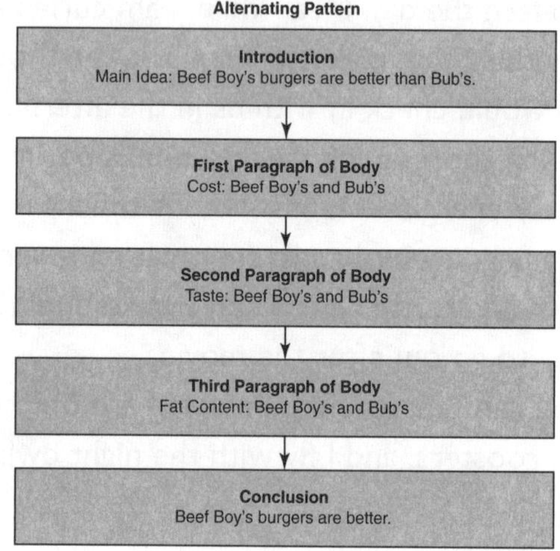

When you write a comparison-and-contrast essay, use transitions to link your ideas.

Comparison-and-Contrast Transitions

in comparison	in the same way	similar to
in contrast	on the other hand	however

Exercise 3

Circle the letter describing the organizing pattern used in the body of each essay.

Main Idea: It is better to pack a lunch than to buy a carry-out lunch.

First, packing lunch saves money. A sandwich, salad, and small drink cost me $9.00 in most take-out places downtown. In contrast, the same lunch costs me only about $3.00 if I make it myself.

I also have more time to relax on my lunch hour when I pack my own lunch. By the time I wait for elevators, traffic lights, and long lines at the restaurant, more than half of my lunch hour is gone. When I bring my lunch, I have plenty of time to sit down and enjoy it.

Finally, I control the ingredients in my lunch when I bring it myself. I use low-fat, low-salt meats and cheeses. In addition, I always include fruit and vegetables. My homemade lunches are far healthier than the average carry-out lunch.

(a) block pattern
(b) alternating pattern

Main Idea: The city at night looks very different from the city during the day.

During the day, the view from my window is exciting. Below me is the hustle and bustle of a great city. Honking cars are jammed at the traffic light. Buses packed with people slowly make their way from stop to stop. Men and women scurry across the street on their way to work.

At night, the view from my window is peaceful. All the hustle and bustle of the day is gone. A lone car pulls away from the traffic light, which has just turned green. A bus with only a few passengers hurries by. The sidewalks are empty, except for a couple walking arm in arm.

(a) block pattern
(b) alternating pattern

Check your answers on page 188.

Read a Comparison-and-Contrast Essay

You have studied three elements of comparison-and-contrast essays: reasons for making comparisons and contrasts, bases of comparison, and patterns of organization. Look for these elements as you read the following essay.

If you have pets—or children or neighbors or coworkers—you probably compare and contrast them. Thinking about similarities and differences helps you notice details.

Like Cats and Dogs

(1) Would you rather own a dog or a cat? If you are like me, you may decide to own one of each. Cats and dogs are different, but they are both fun.

(2) Most obviously, cats and dogs are different sizes. My cat, Flossie, is a petite 16 pounds, while my dog, Thurber, is a massive 60 pounds. Flossie can squeeze into small spaces—for example, in my attic—to search for mice. But because of his size, Thurber would never fit into those spaces. He can only hope to scare mice with his fierce bark.

(3) Flossie moves silently, with a grace that a ballerina would envy. She leaps effortlessly from the floor to the back of the sofa and then to the windowsill. She never disturbs the flowerpot on the sill. On the other hand, Thurber is a little clumsy in the house. He often bumps into chairs and table legs, and nothing breakable is safe when he is around. However, he can speed across a field like a runaway freight train, while Flossie is still trying to choose an acceptable route across the field.

(4) When it comes to eating and drinking habits, the two are miles apart. Flossie is a picky eater. Her food must be soft and fresh. Flossie prefers one brand of canned food over all others. She has been known to ignore food that does not meet her high standards. She refuses to drink water from her bowl. Instead she laps up water from a running faucet. Thurber eats pretty much anything that I put into his bowl. In fact, he does not limit himself to the food in his bowl. From sad experience, I know that he will eat candy, cookies, popcorn, sandwiches, and expensive nut breads that are left within reach. When it comes to drinking, his standards are also low. He will drink water from just about anywhere, including a puddle or a toilet bowl.

LANGUAGE Tip

Punctuation

Notice the use of dashes in paragraph 2 of the passage. Dashes often point to an example. Sometimes they are used to show that a definition follows.

(5) Flossie is particular about where she sleeps. She likes a soft spot, such as a sofa, a pillow, or a bed. If the spot is warm, she likes it even more. She doesn't seem to care whether she is near one of her humans when she naps. In contrast, Thurber does not look for a soft spot when he wants to nap. Maybe that is because he is too big to fit on top of a pillow and is not allowed on the sofa. He dozes on the floor next to whichever person he can find.

(6) Flossie is a dignified animal. She never performs silly tricks for my pleasure. No bribe or treat will induce her to sit up, roll over, shake hands, or play dead on command. In comparison, Thurber is more than willing to sacrifice his pride for a dog biscuit. He will shake hands fifty times if that is what he has to do just to get one small treat. He seems to love both the biscuit and the person who gives it to him.

(7) Does Flossie love me? It is hard to say for sure. She ignores me for long stretches of time. During most of the day, she is busy grooming herself, taking naps, and looking out the window. It is only at mealtimes that she seems to remember me. Then she circles my legs and meows until I fill her bowl. Only at nighttime does she sit on my lap or nestle at the foot of my bed. In contrast, Thurber follows me around the house. He seems to hate being alone. He is always ready to play fetch with me. When I come back home after being away for even a few minutes, Thurber greets me with excitement. I am lucky if Flossie looks my way when I come home.

(8) Flossie's lack of interest in human activity makes her useless as a watch cat. If a burglar ever entered my home, she would probably open one eye and then go back to sleep. Thurber, on the other hand, would bark and attack to defend everyone in the house. For a mild-mannered dog, he can look and act ferocious when the need arises.

(9) In a surprising twist, if there were a face-off between Flossie and Thurber, I would always bet on Flossie. In spite of her smaller size, she can back Thurber into a corner and transform him from a figure of strength into a whimpering loser.

(10) I enjoy living with both of these animals. My life would be much less exciting if it weren't for my cat and dog.

Check Your Understanding

PART A

Answer each question about "Like Cats and Dogs." Look back at the essay if you need to.

1. What point is the author trying to make by comparing and contrasting? Circle the letter of the correct answer.
   (a) to show that her cat and dog differ
   (b) to show that a cat is a better pet than a dog

2. Circle all bases of comparison that the author used to compare and contrast her cat and dog.

size	attachment to humans
color	ability to defend against burglars
sleeping habits	style of movement
eating habits	moods
life spans	intelligence

3. Which pattern of organization did the author use? Circle the letter of the correct answer.
   (a) block method
   (b) alternating method

PART B

Answer each question in a sentence or two.

1. Copy the main-idea sentence from the introduction.

   ____

2. Describe another way that cats and dogs often differ. Describe a way that they are alike.

   ____

   ____

   ____

Check your answers on page 188.

Write a Comparison-and-Contrast Essay

Prewriting: Selecting a Topic and a Purpose

The author of "Like Cats and Dogs" compares and contrasts two pets. Write an essay that compares and contrasts two people, groups, places, or things. Your purpose is to explain. The topic you choose to describe could be

- two people you know well
- men and women
- yourself at two different times of your life
- different ways of accomplishing a goal
- a favorite place at different times of the year
- two brands of the same product

Below are some ideas to get you started. Choose *one* of these topics or use a topic of your own. Check your journal for ideas. You may have written about people, places, or things that you would enjoy comparing and contrasting in an essay.

- two of your children
- your current boyfriend or girlfriend and your former boyfriend or girlfriend
- men's and women's attitudes toward a particular subject
- eating at home and eating in a restaurant
- watching a sporting event on TV and seeing the event in person
- sewing an item of clothing and buying an item ready-made
- your town's downtown area on a weekday and on Sunday
- your favorite brand of ice cream and another brand

Write your topic here.

Topic: ____

Prewriting: Developing Your Topic

Now that you have your topic, you need to think of bases of comparison so you can develop the topic. To decide which qualities to compare and contrast, think about your topic and main idea. Ask yourself, "What point do I want to make by comparing and contrasting? Do I want to show that one thing is better than another? Or do I simply want to describe similarities and differences?" The answers to these questions will help you decide which qualities to write about.

Here is a comparison-and-contrast chart completed by a student.

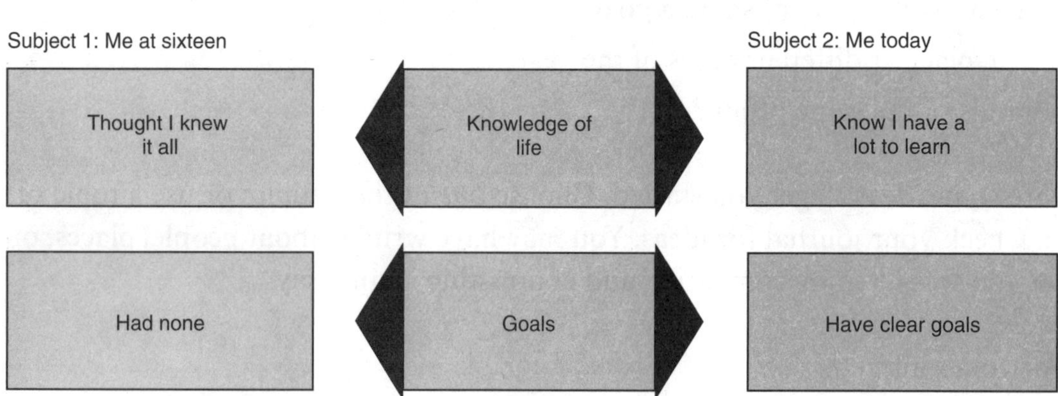

Now fill in the bank chart, describing the two people, places, or things you have chosen. You do not have to use all the bases of comparison. If you wish, you may add more bases of comparison.

COMPARISON-AND-CONTRAST CHART

Subject 1: ________________

Subject 2: ________________

Prewriting: Organizing Your Ideas

Finish prewriting by organizing your ideas.

Write a main-idea sentence.

Put your main idea in sentence form.

Main-idea sentence: ____

____

Group your bases of comparison.

Which pattern of organization will you use—block or alternating? If you have only one or two bases of comparison, the block method will probably work well for you. If you have three or more bases, the alternating pattern may be a better choice.

The student who made the chart decided to use the block method because she had only two bases of comparison. Which pattern of organization will you use? **Write the pattern you will use here.**

Pattern of organization: ____

You may also find it helpful to map your essay. If you are using the block method of organization, follow the student's example below. If you're using the alternating pattern, look back at page 100 for an example.

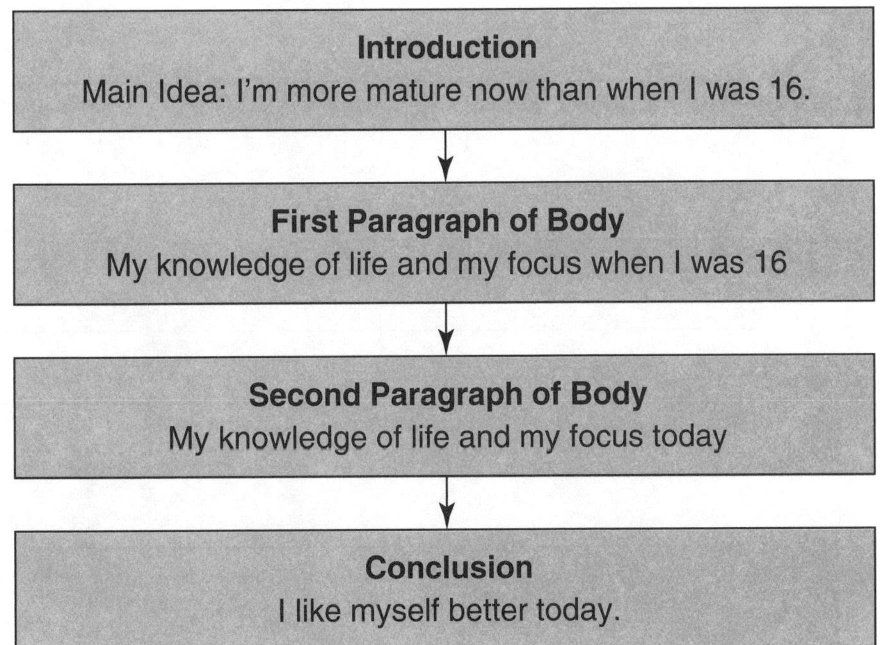

Introduction
Main Idea: I'm more mature now than when I was 16.
First Paragraph of Body
My knowledge of life and my focus when I was 16
Second Paragraph of Body
My knowledge of life and my focus today
Conclusion
I like myself better today.

Drafting

The next stage of the writing process is drafting. During this stage, you use your prewriting plan to write a first draft. Remember that a first draft is just a first try. You will have a chance to improve your writing when you revise and edit.

Using your prewriting plan, write a first draft on the topic of your choice. If you need more space, continue writing on a piece of paper.

Include a clear main-idea sentence in the introduction.

Use transitions to introduce bases of comparison.

End by restating the main idea.

Revising

The next stage is to evaluate your first draft. You may do this alone or with a partner. First, do the Revision Warm-Up. Then use the Revision Checklist to revise your draft.

Revision Warm-Up

Follow the directions below.

1. Write an introduction.
2. Add a conclusion that restates the main idea.

Yesterday and Today

I'm more mature now than when I was sixteen.____________________

When I was sixteen, I was a know-it-all. My parents begged me to stay in school, but I ignored them. They seemed so hopelessly out of touch with the world and my life. Now that I am twenty-six, I know my parents were right. As a dropout, I have not been able to get very good jobs. To better myself, I have gone back to school. I know I have a lot to learn.

At sixteen, I had very little focus in life. In fact, I had only two goals. I wanted to get a job so I could buy a nice car and fancy clothes. I also wanted to be friends with the "right" people. In contrast, my goals today are very different. I do not care about fancy clothes or cars. I spend more time with family than with friends. Now I want to get a good education and find a good job.

____

Check your answers on pages 188–189.

☑ Revision Checklist

Yes	No	
❑	❑	**1.** Is there a main-idea sentence in the introduction?
❑	❑	**2.** Do all the bases of comparison support the main idea?
❑	❑	**3.** Are the bases of comparison logically organized?
❑	❑	**4.** Are the ideas linked with transitions?
❑	❑	**5.** Does the conclusion restate the main idea?

Editing

The last stage of the writing process is editing. During this stage, you look for and correct errors in grammar, mechanics, and usage.

Do the Editing Exercise. Then edit the draft of your essay. Look for and correct noun, pronoun, verbs, adjective and adverb, and sentence-structure errors. Also look for other kinds of errors. If possible, work with a partner.

Editing Exercise: Sentence Structure

Underline and correct the nine errors in sentence structure and punctuation.

On My Own

Should I get my own apartment. That was the question I kept asking myself. Finally I decided to go ahead and I rented my own place. Although it is expensive being on my own it is well worth it.

I love the freedom of being independent. I answer to no one, I come and go as I please. If I come in at 3 o'clock in the morning. There is no one yelling at me, asking me where I have been.

I also enjoy my new-found privacy. When I lived at home, my little brother was always poking his nose in my business. I could not talk on the phone to my friends. Without my little brother listening in on our calls. Now my life is much better I am able to keep private things private.

It is expensive to be on my own however I don't mind paying the price. I guess I am just one of those people. Who are better off being on their own.

Check your answers on page 189.

Part II

Grammar

Forming the Past Tense: Irregular Verbs

Irregular verbs do not form the past tense by adding *d* or *ed*. Most irregular verbs form the past tense by a change in spelling. The most irregular verb is *be*.

Singular	Plural
I was	We were
You were	You were
He, she, it was	They were

Here are some other common irregular verbs. More irregular verbs are shown on pages 145–148.

Present	Past	Present	Past	Present	Past
begin(s)	began	go(es)	went	speak(s)	spoke
bring(s)	brought	run(s)	ran	take(s)	took
come(s)	came	see(s)	saw	tell(s)	told
eat(s)	ate	sing(s)	sang	write(s)	wrote

In the blank, write the past tense of the verb in parentheses.

- The Gary Project ___began___ (begin) in 1975.

Folklorists from Indiana University ________ (run) the project. The folklorists ________ (be) interested in old customs. Many people ________ (go) to Gary, Indiana. They ________ (speak) about the culture of their families. The folklorists ________ (see) how families followed traditions. Mrs. Meléndez ________ (tell) the group traditional folk tales. She said her family ________ (eat) only Puerto Rican foods for many years. Philip ________ (write) down what she said. I ________ (be) glad that I attended.

Check your answers on page 194.

Chapter 8

Test Skill

Nouns

Identifying Nouns

A **noun** is a word that names a person, place, thing, or idea.

Person	Mr. Chung, Dan, Aunt Amy, neighbor, politician, child
Place	Alaska, Washington Avenue, store, yard, home, hospital
Thing	*Sound of Music,* Ray's Supermarket, screwdriver, kitten, toy, sofa
Idea	anger, peace, friendship, hope, confusion, wealth, intelligence

PART A

Underline the nouns in each sentence.

- Buffalo Bill got his nickname because he killed many buffaloes.

1. William Cody was born in Iowa.
2. As a young boy, Cody was a rider for the Pony Express.
3. Cody and his wife had four children.
4. Buffalo Bill is most famous for his Wild West Show.
5. More than 1,000 people and their horses opened the show with a parade.
6. Then the actors had a shooting contest and pretended to rob a stagecoach.
7. People saw what the West was like before railroads changed the land.
8. The show traveled all around the world, and Cody even met the Pope.
9. Buffalo Bill is buried in Golden, Colorado.

PART B

Write the name of the person, place, thing, or idea.

1. ____________________ (your street)
2. ____________________ (your state)
3. ____________________ (best friend)
4. ____________________ (favorite food)

Check your answers on page 190.

Capitalizing Nouns I

Capitalize **proper nouns**—specific names of people, places, or things.

Do not capitalize **common nouns**—general names of people, places, or things.

> **LANGUAGE Tip**
>
> The French Quarter is a neighborhood in New Orleans settled by the French in the early 1700s. It is known for restaurants, hotels, and jazz.

Proper nouns	Oprah Winfrey, Horton Hotel, Korean War
Common nouns	woman, hotel, war

Be sure to capitalize all the main parts of a proper noun.

- the Midville Museum of Natural History

Capitalize job and family titles that come directly before a name and are considered part of the name.

- Dr. Wong, President Bush, Aunt Marie

Capitalize the proper nouns in each sentence.

- In 2000, my friend Lee was a student at Louisiana State University at Alexandria.

1. Lee went on a vacation to new orleans.
2. His brother luis was going to tulane university.
3. Lee was amazed by the size of lake pontchartrain.
4. Luis took lee to bourbon street
5. It is in the french quarter, my favorite part of the city.
6. After lunch, the two walked to jackson square.
7. Then the boys caught a streetcar to meet uncle jerome.
8. Uncle jerome was talking to congresswoman jones.
9. The congresswoman left to go back to the hilton hotel.
10. The family went to hear buddy guy, a blues singer.
11. The family also saw a great jazz band at preservation hall.
12. Later the boys went to their uncle's house on paris road.
13. Aunt jana served the fish she'd caught in the mississippi river.
14. Lee was happy he saw the city before hurricane katrina hit in 2005.

Check your answers on page 190.

LANGUAGE Tip

Thanksgiving is celebrated in the United States on the fourth Thursday of November. Many families eat turkey, cranberries, and pumpkin pie on this day.

Capitalizing Nouns II

Capitalize days of the week and months of the year.

- Monday, Friday, January, February

Do not capitalize the seasons of the year.

- spring, summer, winter, fall

Capitalize specific holidays.

- Easter, Thanksgiving, the Fourth of July

PART A

Capitalize the proper nouns in each sentence.

- I think holidays should occur on Mondays or Fridays.

1. If thanksgiving were on monday, all the cooking could be done over the weekend.
2. Trick-or-treating on friday night would make halloween easier on parents.
3. Couples could sleep late on saturday after a valentine's day date on friday night.
4. I wish new year's eve were in may.
5. It is too cold in january to celebrate.
6. The heat of summer might be better for presidents' day.
7. Of course, the cold of winter is perfect for christmas.
8. But birthdays on december 25 should be banned.

PART B

Complete the questionnaire. Be sure to capitalize correctly.

Your address: ______________________________

(street)

____

(city) (state) (ZIP)

Your doctor's name: ______________________________

(first) (last)

Days you work or go to school: ______________________________

Check your answers on page 190.

Identifying Plural Nouns

A **plural noun** names more than one person, place, thing, or idea. Form the plural of most nouns by adding an *s*.

- one girl—two girls
- this room—those rooms

Signal words can tell you if a noun is singular or plural. Some common singular signal words are *one, a, an, each, every, a single, this,* and *that*. Some common plural signal words are *two, both, several, many, these,* and *those.*

- It took three workers to lift that table.

Context (the way a word is used in combination with other words) can also tell you if a noun should be singular or plural. In the following sentence, you can tell that *boys* should be plural because a team consists of more than one boy.

- The boys on the team stay late to practice.

PART A

Circle *S* if the underlined noun is singular or *P* if it is plural.

- S (P) both pets

S P 1. a child

S P 2. four meals

S P 3. every mess

S P 4. several bowls

S P 5. many desserts

PART B

Underline and correct the plural error in each sentence.

- The two boy (boys) set the table.

Hsu put out a stack of napkin for the whole family. Then Mr. Nurachi brought in several bowl of beans. Hsu's mother placed a pair of chopstick by each place. All member of the family sat down to eat.

Check your answers on page 190.

Spelling Regular Plurals

Use these guidelines to spell the plural of **regular nouns.**

Form the plural of nouns that end in *s, sh, ch, x,* and *z* by adding an *es* ending.

- one dress—two dresses
- a match—several matches

Form the plural of nouns that end in a consonant and a *y* by changing *y* to *i* and adding *es*.

- a baby—four babies
- one city—many cities

In some cases, nouns ending in *f* or *fe* form the plural with an *s* ending. In other cases, the plural is formed by changing the *f* or *fe* to *v* and adding *es*.

- this safe—these safes
- a knife—both knives

Form the plural of nouns ending in a vowel and an *o* by adding *s*. Form the plural of most nouns ending in a consonant and an *o* by adding *es*.

- her stereo—their stereos
- that potato—those potatoes

Underline the correct plural form in parentheses.

- Cesar Chavez is one of my (heros, heroes).

1. His work changed the (lifes, lives) of many migrant workers.
2. With the help of union (attorneys, attornies), Chavez organized a strike against grape growers.
3. Many (familys, families) in the United States refused to buy grapes.
4. People left lettuce on grocery store (shelfs, shelves).
5. (Churchs, Churches) across the nation supported the boycott.
6. Now many migrant workers, such as those who pick (tomatos, tomatoes), have contracts.
7. What are your (beliefs, believes) about boycotts?
8. Should people boycott (companys, companies) they dislike?

Check your answers on page 190.

Spelling Irregular Plurals

Irregular nouns do not follow the rules for forming noun plurals. Use these guidelines to spell the plurals of irregular nouns.

For some irregular nouns, the plural form is the same as the singular form.

- a deer—several deer
- one fish—two fish

Some irregular nouns have only a plural form.

- scissors, eyeglasses, pants, clothes

The plural of some irregular nouns is formed by changing the spelling of the noun.

- one woman—two women
- every child—many children
- this tooth—those teeth
- a mouse—several mice

In the blank, write the plural of the noun in parentheses.

- A group of ___children___ made a mural.

1. (scissors) They used ________________ to cut animal shapes.
2. (fish) They drew pictures of birds and ________________.
3. (mouse) Some kids painted pictures of ________________.
4. (tooth) One boy drew only the animals' ________________.
5. (glasses) One girl drew ________________ on her elephant.
6. (foot) A funny cow had only three ________________.
7. (clothes) More paint got on ________________ than on the paper.
8. (pants) Two kids ruined their shirts and ________________.
9. (person) Many ________________ came to see the mural.
10. (woman) The two ________________ who ran the school were proud.

Check your answers on page 190.

Forming Singular Possessives

A **possessive noun** shows ownership or relationship. Use these guidelines to form **singular possessives.**

Form the possessive of singular nouns by adding an apostrophe (') and an *s*.

- John's book is missing. (The book belongs to John.)
- The man's wife called. (The wife of the man called.)

Even when a singular noun ends in *s*, add *'s* to form the possessive.

- Mr. Santos's book is on the table.

PART A

Change each underlined noun to a singular possessive.

- Mrs. Pallas just read that writer's second novel.

1. The authors name is Amy Tan.
2. Tans book is about a mother and a daughter.
3. The mothers part of the story is set in China.
4. Mrs. Pallass favorite chapter is at the end of the book.
5. The older woman reveals a secret about her daughters past.
6. The novels title is *The Kitchen God's Wife*.

PART B

Using a possessive noun, rewrite the phrase in parentheses. Be sure to put the apostrophe where it belongs.

- the writer's house ________ (the house of the writer)

1. ________ (the plot of the novel)
2. ________ (the interest of the reader)
3. ________ (the cover of the book)
4. ________ (the ideas of the student)

Check your answers on pages 190–191.

Forming Plural Possessives

Form the possessive of regular plural nouns by adding an apostrophe (') after the *s*.

- the twins' room
- the Sanchezes' apartment
- many companies' problcms

PART A

Change each underlined noun to a plural possessive.

- Our landlords often ignore their renters' troubles.

1. Last night we held a tenants meeting.
2. We all met in the Golds apartment.
3. Mrs. Gold made a list of the families complaints.
4. The Schwartzes complaint was about their plumbing.
5. The Schramms complained about their windows broken latches.
6. The Smiths problem was a broken door lock.
7. I said that our two bedrooms electrical sockets were unsafe.
8. Maybe a letter will get those landlords attention.

PART B

Using a possessive noun, rewrite the phrase in parentheses. Be sure to put the apostrophe where it belongs.

- *the ladies' hats* ______ (the hats of the ladies)

1. ______________________ (the cases of the attorneys)
2. ______________________ (the products of several companies)
3. ______________________ (the complaints of the clients)

Check your answers on page 191.

Forming Irregular Possessives

To form the possessive of plural nouns that do not end in *s*, add an apostrophe (') and an *s*.

- the men's fashions
- people's preferences

PART A

Using a possessive noun, rewrite the phrase in parentheses. Be sure to put the apostrophe where it belongs.

- the men's job ______ (the job of the men)

1. ______ (the boats of the fishermen)
2. ______ (the toys of the children)
3. ______ (the uniforms of the women)
4. ______ (the tails of those mice)
5. ______ (the choice of the people)

PART B

This is a review of the possessive noun rules. Underline the possessive noun in each sentence. Then add the apostrophe in the correct place.

- My town's public library is excellent.

The librarys collection of books and magazines is impressive. The friendly staff works hard to meet peoples needs. The childrens room has books, magazines, CDs, DVDs, and computers. The room has won many parents praise.

Check your answers on page 191.

Chapter 8 Review—Nouns

This exercise is a review of the rules you have studied in this chapter. Underline and correct the noun error in each sentence.

- The World's Fair held in Chicago in 1893 was called the Columbian Exposition.

LANGUAGE Tip

The first World's Fair was in London in 1851. Here is a list of 21st-century World's Fairs:

2000	Germany
2005	Japan
2008	Spain
2010	China

1. The fairgrounds were located about eight miles south of chicago.
2. A fires in 1871 had destroyed much of Chicago, but the city rebuilt itself.
3. Almost 200 Buildings were built for the fair.
4. The dedication ceremonys were held in October 1892.
5. About 10,000 man worked to finish the buildings and gardens in time for the grand opening.
6. People were excited when the fair opened in may 1893.
7. Special train tracks' were laid to bring people to the fair.
8. The fair was on the shore of lake Michigan, so some people arrived by boat.
9. Displayes from 46 countries showed what life was like around the world.
10. For the first time ever, electric Street lights were used.
11. Strange new machines showed movieses for the first time.
12. Other new things at the fair included Cracker jacks and Juicy Fruit gum.
13. But the most exciting invention was a huge wheel created by George Ferris'.
14. The Ferris wheel had 36 cars, and each car could carry 60 peoples.
15. Mr. Ferris wife wanted to be on the first Ferris wheel ride.
16. The fair was closed on sundays.
17. About 27 million people attended the fair, including the president of the united States.

Check your answers on page 191.

Chapter 9

Test Skill

Pronouns

Identifying Pronouns

A **pronoun** is a word that can replace a noun. Pronouns can be singular or plural.

- The lock is broken. I will fix it. (*It* replaces *lock*.)
- I need new keys. I will buy them. (*Them* replaces *keys*.)

First-person pronouns refer to the person who is speaking in a sentence.
Second-person pronouns refer to the person being spoken to.
Third-person pronouns refer to the person or thing being spoken about.

	Singular	**Plural**
First person	I, me, my, mine, myself	we, us, our, ours, ourselves
Second person	you, your, yours, yourself	you, your, yours, yourself
Third person	he, him, his, himself she, her, hers, herself it, its, itself	they, them, their, theirs, themselves

Underline the pronouns in each sentence.

- Lucille Ball and her husband Desi Arnez became famous because of their TV show *I Love Lucy.*

1. They played the parts of a husband and wife living in a small apartment.
2. They brought laughter to our homes every Monday night for six years.
3. For four of the years, it was the most popular TV show in America.
4. Americans recognized themselves in Lucy and Desi.
5. Lucy is known for her red hair, big eyes, and funny facial expressions.
6. She began her acting career in movies and on the radio.
7. At first, TV producers were not interested in Desi because of his Spanish accent.
8. You have probably seen *I Love Lucy* reruns, so you know how funny they are.
9. My favorite episode shows Lucy stuffing her mouth with candy while working in a chocolate factory.

Check your answers on page 191.

Using Subject Pronouns

Subject pronouns take the place of subject nouns. The **subject** is the person, place, thing, or idea that a sentence is about.

- Ed called. He left a message. (*He* replaces the subject noun *Ed.*)
- Sewing is easy. It is fun. (*It* replaces the subject noun *sewing.*)

The subject pronouns are *I, you, he, she, it, we,* and *they*.

PART A

In the parentheses, write the pronoun that correctly replaces the underlined subject noun or nouns.

- Linda (____She____) is reading a new book.

1. Tony Hillerman (____________) wrote the mystery novel.
2. The novel (____________) is about a Navaho detective, Jim Chee.
3. Jim Chee (____________) investigates a woman's disappearance.
4. The woman (____________) knew a secret about some thieves.
5. The thieves (____________) were afraid the woman would tell.
6. Linda and I (____________) think the thieves killed the woman.
7. Do you and Al (____________) know how the novel ends?
8. Guessing the ending (____________) is part of the fun.

PART B

Write a sentence for each pronoun in parentheses.

- (we) We are planning a party

1. (I) ____
2. (she) ____
3. (they) ____
4. (it) ____

Check your answers on page 191.

Using Object Pronouns I

Object pronouns take the place of **object nouns**. The **direct object** receives the action in a sentence.

- Tim kissed her. (Who received the kiss? *Her*)

The **indirect object** receives the direct object.

- She gave him her love. (Who received her love? *Him*)

The object pronouns are *me, you, him, her, it, us,* and *them.*

LANGUAGE Tip

Jazz is a mixture of West African, classical, and religious music. Jazz has strong rhythms. Often band members make up their music as they play along with a soloist.

PART A

In the parentheses, write the pronoun that correctly replaces the underlined object noun or nouns.

- I first heard Louis Armstrong (___him___) play jazz in 1964.

1. A recording of "Hello Dolly!" brought Armstrong (__________) to my attention.
2. My parents bought my brother and me (__________) the record.
3. I played that record and others (__________) for Jess and Tom.
4. They hadn't heard jazz (__________) before.
5. Tom's mother asked Jess, Tom, and me (__________) why we liked jazz.
6. We couldn't give Mrs. Sanders (__________) an answer.
7. We asked Tom's mom (__________) to listen to our records.
8. She said that she liked the songs (__________).
9. I will lend you and your friends (__________) the records.
10. I am sure that you will enjoy the music (__________).

PART B

Write a sentence for each pronoun in parentheses.

- (me) *George taught me how to play the piano.*

1. (him) ______________________________
2. (her) ______________________________
3. (us) ______________________________

Check your answers on pages 191–192.

Using Object Pronouns II

Pronouns that follow prepositions also take the object form. These pronouns are called **objects of the preposition.**

- Give it to me. (*Me* is the object of the preposition *to.*)

Common Prepositions

about	beside	from	to
after	between	in	toward
against	by	near	under
at	except	on	with
behind	for	over	without

PART A

In the parentheses, write the pronoun that correctly replaces the underlined object or objects of the preposition.

- Mr. West will take a picture of the club members (____them____).

1. We will start the picture taking without Mary (____________).
2. Martha, will you stand over by Bill (____________)?
3. John, please sit in the first chair (____________).
4. Della, you should move near Harry and Bill (____________).
5. Mrs. Romero, please stand beside Ellen and me (____________).
6. Take Mr. Samms with Fred and you (____________).
7. Will someone turn the light toward the last row (____________)?
8. Everyone smile and look at the camera (____________).

PART B

This is a review of the object pronoun rules. Underline and correct the pronoun error in each sentence.

- The instructor gave ~~we~~ us a writing assignment.

He asked I to read my essay aloud. He also asked Yolanda to read her essay to he.

Then he gave she helpful advice.

Check your answers on page 192.

Using Pronouns in Compounds

Subjects joined by *and, nor,* or *or* are called **compound subjects.** A pronoun in a compound subject takes the subject form.

- Okei and (I, me) work at a computer store.

Objects joined by *and, nor,* or *or* are called **compound objects.** A pronoun in a compound object takes the object form.

- Lunch is at 1:30 p.m. for Okei and (I, me).

If you have trouble deciding which form to use, read each part of the compound separately.

- Okei works at a computer store. I work at a computer store.
- Lunch is at 1:30 p.m. for Okei. Lunch is at 1:30 p.m. for me.

> **LANGUAGE Tip**
>
> *Grammar*
>
> When talking about yourself and someone else, always name yourself last.
>
> Rea **and I** like ice tea.
>
> The taxi took him **and me** to the station.

PART A

Underline the correct pronoun in parentheses.

- Have you and (she, her) tried the new Korean restaurant?

1. Okei and (I, me) went there last week.
2. (She, Her) and I had hot rice dishes.
3. The owner's wife waited on my friend and (I, me).
4. We told John and (he, him) about the place.
5. John asked Roger and (we, us) to meet there yesterday.
6. (We, Us) and (they, them) ate a spicy soup and seafood.
7. I thanked Okei and (they, them) for a pleasant meal.

PART B

Underline and correct the compound subject or compound object error in each sentence.

- Mr. Takei and her (she) like Mexican food.

Neither their children nor them know how to cook it. The children often take he and her out to eat. You and me should go with them sometime.

Check your answers on page 192.

Using Possessive Pronouns I

Possessive pronouns are used to show ownership or relationship.

- My dog chased your cat into their yard.

The possessive pronouns are *my, your, his, her, its, our,* and *their*.

Do not confuse these pronoun pairs.

- You're crazy about your cat.
  (You're is short for "you are," and your is a possessive pronoun.)
- They're angry that the dog dug up their yard.
  (They're is short for "they are," and their is a possessive pronoun.)
- It's too bad that the cat hurt its paw.
  (It's is short for "it is," and its is a possessive pronoun.)

PART A

Underline the correct word in parentheses.

- Do (your, you're) parents live close by?

1. Dino and Mikel often write to (their, they're) mother.
2. (They're, Their) planning to visit her this summer.
3. (Its, It's) too expensive to mail them large packages.
4. The post office keeps raising (its, it's) rates.
5. How often do you see (your, you're) parents?
6. (Your, You're) lucky if you can visit them once a week.

PART B

Write a sentence for each possesive pronoun in parentheses.

- (my) My vacation starts in a few days.

1. (your) ______________________________
2. (his) ______________________________
3. (its) ______________________________
4. (their) ______________________________

Check your answers on page 192.

Using Possessive Pronouns II

Some possessive pronouns can stand alone. These pronouns are *mine, yours, his, hers, its, ours,* and *theirs.* All of these pronouns end in *s* except *mine.*

- That car is hers. You can borrow mine.

Notice that possessive pronouns do not have apostrophes.

PART A

Underline the pronoun in parentheses that correctly replaces the underlined words.

- Is your dentist in the same building as my dentist?
  (mine, mines)

1. My dentist is Dr. Carmen Rivera, a family friend.
   (Mine, Mines)
2. Do you remember the phone number of your dentist?
   (your, yours)
3. Dr. Rivera's office is on the top floor of the complex.
   (Hers, Her's)
4. My other dentists' offices are on the first floor.
   (Theirs, Their's)
5. If you don't like your dentist, try our family dentist.
   (our, ours)

PART B

In the parentheses, write the possessive pronoun that correctly replaces the underlined words.

- I think this car is Mrs. Garcia's (___*hers*___).

1. I know it isn't the Jones family's car (____________).
2. Their car looks like the car I own (____________).
3. This one looks more like Jim's (____________).
4. May I borrow your car (____________)?

Check your answers on page 192.

Using Reflexive Pronouns

A **reflexive pronoun** directs the action back to the subject. Reflexive pronouns always refer to the subject of the sentence.

- He taught himself to play guitar.
- The cat groomed itself.

Singular	Plural
Singular reflexive pronouns end in *self.*	Plural reflexive pronouns end in *selves.*
myself	ourselves
yourself	yourselves
himself, herself, itself	themselves

Do not use a reflexive pronoun when a subject pronoun or an object pronoun is needed.

Incorrect: He wants Don and yourself to help.
Correct: He wants Don and you to help.

Do not use *hisself* or *theirselves*. These are not correct forms.

Underline the correct pronoun form in parentheses.

- The Bozarths pride (theirselves, themselves) on their ability to do home repairs.

1. I would hurt (me, myself) if I did something like that.
2. Don Bozarth taught (hisself, himself) about plumbing.
3. The kids put (theirselves, themselves) to work painting.
4. Don helped (them, themselves) set up the ladders.
5. Beth told Mr. Silvera and (me, myself) about it yesterday.
6. The Bozarths say the house is practically rebuilding (itself, itselfs).
7. Mr. Silvera and (I, myself) are going over there.
8. Why don't (you, yourself) and Ellen come with us?
9. Get (yourselfs, yourselves) ready.
10. Ellen got (her, herself) out to the car in two minutes.

Check your answers on page 192.

Using Demonstrative Pronouns

Demonstrative pronouns (*this, that, these, those*) are used to point out persons or things. *This* and *that* are singular. *These* and *those* are plural.

This and *these* refer to people and things that are close in time or space.

- This past year has been a good one for me.
- These presents in my hand are yours.

That and *those* refer to people and things that are farther away in time or space.

- Mario will never forget that awful morning last week.
- That house across the street is an eyesore.
- Those weeds in the back need to be pulled.

Do not use the expression *this here* or *that there*. Do not use *them* in place of *those*.

PART A

Underline the correct pronoun form in parentheses.

- (This, This here) is the village where Abraham Lincoln worked as a young shopkeeper.

1. Is (that, that there) the place where he once grew a garden?
2. (Them, Those) paths are the ones Lincoln walked every day.
3. If you want to understand Lincoln, you should visit (that there, that) village.
4. (These, These here) directions will show you the way to Salem, Illinois.
5. (This here, This) village has been rebuilt to look like it did in the 1800s.

PART B

Write a sentence for each demonstrative pronoun in parentheses.

- (this) I have a lot to do this week.

1. (that) ____________________
2. (these) ____________________
3. (those) ____________________

Check your answers on pages 192–193.

Chapter 9 Review—Pronouns

This exercise is a review of the rules you have studied in this chapter. Underline the correct word in parentheses.

- Yellowstone is (your, you're) park because it is a national park.

1. (Its, It's) best known because of Old Faithful.
2. (This, This here) is a geyser that shoots water 130 feet into the air.
3. Early explorers gave Old Faithful (its, it's) name.
4. Hundreds of people gather every 90 minutes so (they, them) can watch Old Faithful go off.
5. They write postcards to (their, they're) friends telling about the park.
6. For many of (them, they), Old Faithful is what makes Yellowstone special.
7. Rangers tell visitors about Old Faithful, and (they, them) know about other geysers too.
8. My family and (I, me) like to stay at Old Faithful Lodge.
9. Bears, bison, moose, and elk make (theirselves, themselves) at home in Yellowstone.
10. (These, These here) animals often look for food left by humans.
11. But this food is not healthy for (they, them).
12. A ranger told (we, us) that snowmobiles scare the animals.
13. (This here, This) is a serious problem.
14. We saw a moose and (her, her's) calf resting near a river.
15. Then the bull moose (himself, hisself) wandered up.
16. He made a loud noise to let us know the family was (his', his).
17. While (I, me) watched the moose, a bear came out of the woods.
18. Has anything like this happened to (you, yourself)?

LANGUAGE Tip

Yellowstone was the first national park in the world. In 1872, more than 2 million acres of wilderness were set aside for people to enjoy. The park is located mostly in the state of Wyoming.

Check your answers on page 193.

Chapter 10

Test Skill

Verbs

Identifying Verbs

A **verb** is a word that shows action.

- Soldiers fight for their country.

A verb can also show a state of being. The verbs used to show state of being are *am, is, are, was, were, be, being,* and *been.*

- They are brave.

Verb tenses tell when an action or a state of being takes place. Sometimes a **helping verb** is used together with a **main verb** to form a verb tense. Some common helping verbs are *has, have, had, am, is, are, was,* and *were.*

- The soldiers have left the base.

Underline the verbs in each sentence.

- In 1991, the war in the Persian Gulf raised an old question.

1. What is a woman's role in the military?
2. A few women had enlisted during World War I.
3. They worked as clerks for Marine headquarters.
4. During World War II, women's reserves were formed.
5. Many people know about military nurses.
6. Women have served in all branches of the military since World War II.
7. A 1948 law banned women from active combat.
8. In 1992, Congress changed the law.
9. Today women can hold combat jobs.
10. More than 200,000 women are serving on land, at sea, and in the air.
11. American women are proud members of the U.S. Armed Forces.

Check your answers on page 193.

Understanding Agreement

The **present tense** is used to show that something happens regularly.

- The sun rises in the east and sets in the west.
- Mr. and Mrs. Thomas sing in the choir every Sunday.

Present tense verbs must **agree** with the subject. A subject and verb agree if they are both singular or both plural.

	Singular	Plural
First person	I work	We work
Second person	You work	You work
Third person	He, she, it works	They work

Notice that when the subject of a sentence is *he, she,* or *it,* the verb must end in *s.*

- He walks. She talks. It barks.

PART A

Underline the correct verb form in parentheses.

- We (study, studies) together on Friday nights.

1. Usually we (meet, meets) at Sarah's house.
2. She always (serve, serves) fruit and nuts as snacks.
3. I (drive, drives) Yolanda and Mario to the study group.
4. They (live, lives) several miles away.
5. You (know, knows) Mario.
6. At each meeting, he (quiz, quizzes) us on our lessons.
7. He (catch, catches) our mistakes.
8. The mistakes (confuse, confuses) me sometimes.
9. The study group really (help, helps) everyone.
10. We (learn, learns) a lot from each other.

Check your answers on page 193.

Understanding Subject Nouns

When the subject of a sentence is the pronoun *he, she,* or *it,* the verb must end in *s*. To tell what verb form to use with a **noun subject**, replace the noun with a pronoun. In the following sentence, for example, *Maria* can be replaced by *she*. Therefore, *works* is the correct verb form.

- Maria (work, works) for an accounting firm. (She works . . .)

In this sentence, *bosses* can be replaced by *they*. Therefore, *think* is the correct verb form.

- Her bosses (think, thinks) highly of her. (They think . . .)

PART A

Write the pronoun that correctly replaces the underlined noun subject. Then underline the correct verb form in parentheses.

- Sports figures (get, gets) lots of attention. They

1. Tiger Woods (play, plays) professional golf.
2. This golfer (win, wins) a lot of tournaments.
3. Woods usually (hit, hits) the ball straight down the fairway.
4. Many fans (watch, watches) the tournaments he plays in on TV.
5. My mother (see, sees) Woods in car commercials.
6. The athlete (give, gives) money to a foundation.
7. The Tiger Woods Foundation (support, supports) children's programs.
8. Children (admire, admires) Woods.
9. The man (set, sets) a good example for other athletes.
10. Some people (call, calls) him the best golfer in the world.
11. This talented man (try, tries) hard.
12. My sisters and I (love, loves) to watch him play.

Check your answers on page 193.

Using *Be, Have,* and *Do*

The chart below shows how to use *be, have,* and *do* correctly in the present tense.

	Singular	**Plural**
First person	I am, have, do	We are, have, do
Second person	You are, have, do	You are, have, do
Third person	He is, has, does She is, has, does It is, has, does	They are, have, do

In the blank, write the present tense of the verb in parentheses.

- Rhode Island ____is____ (be) the smallest state.

1. It ____________ (be) only one-sixth the size of Hawaii.
2. Rhode Island ____________ (have) only about 1 million residents.
3. It ____________ (have) two representatives in the House of Representatives.
4. The coastal cities ____________ (be) home to many people who like to sail.
5. Rhode Islanders ____________ (do) excellent work as jewelry makers.
6. Alaskans ____________ (be) proud to live in the biggest state.
7. Alaska ____________ (be) more than twice as large as Texas.
8. Citizens ____________ (have) a special oil tax paid to them each year.
9. The state ____________ (have) the nickname "The Land of the Midnight Sun."
10. Sled-dog racing is something many people ____________ (do) in the winter.

Check your answers on page 193.

Looking at Questions and Compounds

When you ask a question, part of the verb often comes before the subject. In the examples below, notice that the verb *is* agrees with the subject *dictionary* and that the verb *do* agrees with the subject *you*.

- Is the dictionary on the table?
- Do you ever use it?

LANGUAGE Tip

The mainland of the United States has four time zones: Eastern, Central, Mountain, and Pacific. In addition, there is the Alaskan Time Zone and the Hawaiian Time Zone.

Compound subjects joined by *and* are plural. They need a verb that agrees with a plural subject.

- Gus and Connie are in night school.

When a compound subject is joined by *or* or *nor,* the verb agrees with the subject that is closer to the verb.

- Neither the students nor the tutor works on Fridays.

Underline the correct verb form in parentheses.

- (Are, Is) daylight saving time (DST) confusing for you?

1. (Do, Does) you and your wife always remember to change your clocks?
2. Often my mother and father (forgets, forget) about changing their clocks.
3. What (are, is) the reason for daylight saving time?
4. Saving energy and having longer evenings (are, is) the reasons for DST.
5. My grandmother and grandfather (do, does) not like daylight saving time.
6. Either Congress or the states (are, is) able to pass laws about time changes.
7. Neither Hawaii nor Arizona (change, changes) to daylight saving time.
8. (Do, Does) Americans and Canadians change their clocks on the same day?
9. Neither Nigeria nor Japan (uses, use) daylight saving time.
10. (Are, Is) you on time when clocks spring ahead in March?
11. (Has, Have) you ever changed your clock in the wrong direction?
12. What (are, is) your opinion about having daylight saving time all year round?

Check your answers on page 193.

LANGUAGE Tip

A sharecropper farms land owned by someone else. The sharecropper uses the seeds and tools of the landowner. When the crops are sold, the sharecropper receives part of the profit.

Forming the Past Tense: Regular Verbs

The **past tense** of a verb shows that something has already happened. Form the past tense of **regular verbs** by adding a *d* or *ed* ending. If a verb ends in a consonant and *y*, change the *y* to *i* before adding *ed*.

- All last year, Raul walk<u>ed</u> to work.
- After a while, he hate<u>d</u> the walk.
- He usually carri<u>ed</u> an umbrella.

If you have trouble deciding whether a verb should be in the past tense, watch for time clues—words that show when an action occurred. Past-tense time clues include words such as *yesterday, last year,* and *awhile ago.*

In the blank, write the past tense of the verb in parentheses.

- I ____wondered____ (wonder) about the origin of hair straighteners.

1. Last week I ____________ (decide) to research the subject.
2. I ____________ (learn) about Sarah Breedlove, an African American woman.
3. The sharecropper's daughter ____________ (marry) at fourteen.
4. For years, Breedlove ____________ (wash) clothes for a living.
5. In 1905, Breedlove ____________ (start) her own business.
6. She ____________ (rename) herself Madame C. J. Walker.
7. Madame Walker ____________ (mix) various shampoos and oils.
8. The formulas ____________ (straighten) curly hair.
9. Her products ____________ (change) African American hair styles.

Check your answers on page 194.

Forming the Past Tense: Irregular Verbs

Irregular verbs do not form the past tense by adding *d* or *ed*. Most irregular verbs form the past tense by a change in spelling. The most irregular verb is *be*.

Singular	**Plural**
I was	We were
You were	You were
He, she, it was	They were

Here are some other common irregular verbs. More irregular verbs are shown on pages 145–148.

Present	Past	Present	Past	Present	Past
begin(s)	began	go(es)	went	speak(s)	spoke
bring(s)	brought	run(s)	ran	take(s)	took
come(s)	came	see(s)	saw	tell(s)	told
eat(s)	ate	sing(s)	sang	write(s)	wrote

In the blank, write the past tense of the verb in parentheses.

- The Gary Project ____began____ (begin) in 1975.

Folklorists from Indiana University __________ (run) the project. The folklorists __________ (be) interested in old customs. Many people __________ (go) to Gary, Indiana. They __________ (speak) about the culture of their families. The folklorists __________ (see) how families followed traditions. Mrs. Meléndez __________ (tell) the group traditional folk tales. She said her family __________ (eat) only Puerto Rican foods for many years. Philip __________ (write) down what she said. I __________ (be) glad that I attended.

Check your answers on page 194.

Forming the Future Tense

The **future tense** shows that something will happen at a later date. The future tense of all verbs is formed with the helping verb *will* and a main verb.

- I will be at home tonight.
- He will come to my house next week.
- Soon we will have the arrangements ready.

Time clues that can help you recognize the future tense include *tomorrow, next year,* and *a week from now.*

PART A

In the blank, write the future tense of the verb in parentheses.

- Tomorrow the Gonzales family ___will leave___ (leave) for Mexico.

1. They __________ (stop) in Brownsville on the way.
2. Maria and Carlo __________ (join) them there.
3. Next week the family __________ (be) in Mexico City.
4. Soon little Linda __________ (meet) her grandmother.
5. They all __________ (do) many interesting things.
6. In two weeks, the family __________ (return) home.

PART B

Write a sentence for each verb in parentheses. In each sentence, use one of the time clues listed at the top of this page.

- (go) Tomorrow I will go shopping.

1. (win) __________
2. (learn) __________
3. (make) __________

Check your answers on page 194.

Forming the Continuous Tenses

The **continuous tenses** are used to show actions that are in progress.

The **present continuous tense** shows that something is happening at the present time. It is formed by using the helping verb *am, is,* or *are* and a main verb ending in *ing*.

- What are you doing? I am watching TV.

The **past continuous tense** shows that an action took place over a period of time. It is formed by using the helping verb *was* or *were* and a main verb ending in *ing*.

- What were you doing when I called? I was sleeping.

The **future continuous tense** shows that an action will happen in the future. It is formed by using the helping verb *will be* and a main verb ending in *ing*.

- What will you be doing later? I will be studying.

PART A

Underline the correct form of the helping verb in parentheses.

- People (are, is) learning to take better care of themselves.

1. Not long ago, Americans (were, was) becoming couch potatoes.
2. The general health of the nation (were, was) getting worse.
3. Now some people (are, is) taking better care of themselves.
4. I (am, is) walking half an hour each day.
5. (Are, Is) you exercising?
6. Lynn (are, is) watching her children's diet.

PART B

Use the continuous verb form to answer each question.

- Where are you going? I am going to the movies.

1. What are you doing? ______________________
2. What were you doing? ______________________
3. What will you be doing? ______________________

Check your answers on page 194.

LANGUAGE Tip

The movie *The Lion King* was made in 1994. Movie-ticket sales totaled $783 million.

Chapter 10 Review—Verbs

This exercise is a review of the rules you have studied in this chapter. Underline the correct verb form in parentheses.

- As a child, I (love, <u>loved</u>) musicals.

1. Back then, musicals (were, was) often playing at movie theaters.
2. (Are, Is) you old enough to remember them?
3. The stars (were, was) always beautiful and full of energy.
4. Today's actors (lack, lacks) the singing and dancing skill of the old movie stars.
5. When I was growing up, my favorite movie (were, was) *Grease*.
6. John Travolta (dance, danced) like a pro.
7. In the 1990s, musicals (make, made) a comeback with *The Lion King* and *Toy Story*.
8. The catchy songs (delight, delighted) everyone.
9. In the late 1990s, musical hits (fade, faded) from the scene once again.
10. But some studios (are, is) making musicals again.
11. Movies like *Moulin Rouge!* and *Chicago* (were, was) very popular.
12. I (watch, watches) musicals whenever possible.
13. Last week I (rent, rented) *Sweeney Todd: The Demon Barber of Fleet Street*.
14. I have (see, seen) it many times.
15. I also like to (go, gone) to plays such as *Rent* and *Wicked*.
16. I even watch musicals on TV when networks (show, shows) the old classics.
17. (Do, Does) you ever watch classic movies?
18. I (have, has) copies of all my favorites.
19. Will you (watch, watched) a musical with me tonight?

Check your answers on page 194.

Chapter 11

Test Skill

More About Verbs

Using the Present Perfect Tense

An action in the **present perfect tense** begins in the past and continues in the present.

- Mr. Hinojosa has opened his shop at 9:00 a.m. for years.

The present perfect tense can also show that something happened one or more times at an unspecific time in the past.

- Mr. Hinojosa and his wife have visited Canada.

To form the present perfect tense of a regular verb, use the correct form of the helping verb *have* and the past participle of the verb. Form the past participle of regular verbs by adding *d* or *ed* to the main verb.

Do not confuse the present perfect tense with the past tense. Look for time clues that tell which tense to use.

- Last fall, we moved. For the past year, we have enjoyed city life.

Moved happened at a specific time in the past. *Have enjoyed* began in the past and continues in the present.

In the blank, write the correct tense of the verb in parentheses.

- (die) Mrs. Maizel's husband ___died___ ten years ago.

1. (look) Until recently, her house ____________ clean and tidy.
2. (look) But for the past several months, it ____________ sloppy.
3. (notice) Visitors ____________ a musty smell in the house.
4. (complain) Several times people ____________ about her messy yard.
5. (offer) Yesterday our son ____________ to help Mrs. Maizel.
6. (refuse) But the proud woman ____________.

Check your answers on page 194.

LANGUAGE Tip

Baseball was first played in 1845 in New York City. Today there are 30 major-league teams. The World Series is played each October to determine the national champion.

Using the Past Perfect Tense

The **past perfect tense** shows that one past action took place before another past action. To form the past perfect tense of a regular verb, use the helping verb *had* and the past participle of the verb.

- The bus had pulled away by the time Abby got to the station.
- Before the accident, José had wanted to be a football player.

Do not confuse the past perfect tense with other tenses. Use the simple past tense to express an action that took place but no longer continues.

- In May of 2006, I accepted a full-time job at Tool World.

Use the present perfect tense to show that an action started in the past and continues.

- Since then, I have worked my way up to assistant manager.

Underline the correct verb tense in parentheses.

- Lou Gehrig (died, has died) about 70 years ago.

1. He (was, has been) a great baseball player.
2. Before playing for the New York Yankees, he (has played, had played) on high school and college teams.
3. Gehrig (won, had won) the American League's Most Valuable Player award in 1927 and 1936.
4. But after playing 2,130 games in a row, Gehrig (started, has started) to have a hard time moving.
5. Doctors (have discovered, discovered) that he had a nerve disease called ALS.
6. The Yankees (honored, have honored) Gehrig at a ceremony on July 4, 1939.
7. Gehrig said, "I (had received, have received) nothing but kindness from you."
8. People stood and (clapped, have clapped) for two minutes.
9. Doctors (learned, have learned) more about ALS, but they still cannot cure the disease.

Check your answers on pages 194–195.

Using Irregular Verbs I

Irregular verbs do not form the past participle with a *d* or *ed* ending. Here are the present tense, the past tense, and the past participle of some common irregular verbs.

Present	Past	Past Participle
be [am]	was	been
be [is]	was	been
be [are]	were	been
become(s)	became	become
begin(s)	began	begun
blow(s)	blew	blown
break(s)	broke	broken
bring(s)	brought	brought

In the blanks, write the correct tense of the verb in parentheses.

- (begin) Children ___begin___ to walk at various ages. My son ___began___ to walk at 11 months. He had just ___begun___ to walk when he broke his arm.

1. (be) Here ____________ my cats. They ____________ under the bed a few minutes ago. They had ____________ afraid to come out.

2. (become) People ____________ U.S. citizens every day. Keisah ____________ a citizen last month. She has ____________ used to living in the United States.

3. (break) My glasses ____________ easily. I have ____________ them many times. I ____________ them again yesterday.

4. (blow) Every year the wind ____________ leaves into my yard. Last week my neighbor's leaves ____________ into my yard. I wish the wind had ____________ them somewhere else.

5. (bring) Mrs. Arlo always ____________ a dessert. Last Sunday she ____________ a raisin pie. She has often ____________ a home-baked pie.

Check your answers on page 195.

Using Irregular Verbs II

Here are the present tense, the past tense, and the past participle of some other common irregular verbs.

Present	Past	Past Participle
buy(s)	bought	bought
come(s)	came	come
do(es)	did	done
drink(s)	drank	drunk
eat(s)	ate	eaten
freeze(s)	froze	frozen

In the blanks, write the correct tense of the verb in parentheses.

- (buy) I often ___buy___ things on sale. Once I ___bought___ an entire case of hot sauce. I realized I had ___bought___ enough for all my neighbors.

1. (come) He asked, "Why have you ______________ to New York?" I replied, "I ______________ to visit my sister. I ______________ here every fall."

2. (do) Karen ______________ her own taxes each April. Last year she ______________ mine too. She has ______________ Rob's taxes six years in a row.

3. (drink) Mr. Estivez often ______________ too much coffee. Yesterday we ______________ coffee in our favorite café. Before I could finish my first cup, he had ______________ almost a potful.

4. (eat) My dog ______________ too much. Last week he ______________ almost an entire loaf of bread. He has ______________ bread before.

5. (freeze) The local pond ______________ every winter. This morning kids started skating on it as soon as the water had ______________. Last winter the pond ______________ in early November.

Check your answers on page 195.

Using Irregular Verbs III

Here are the present tense, the past tense, and the past participle of another group of common irregular verbs.

Present	Past	Past Participle
give(s)	gave	given
go(es)	went	gone
grow(s)	grew	grown
have (has)	had	had
know(s)	knew	known
run(s)	ran	run
see(s)	saw	seen

In the blanks, write the correct tense of the verb in parentheses.

- (give) Ms. Fu ___gives___ karate lessons on Tuesdays. She ___gave___ me my first lesson in June. Her son had ___given___ me lessons before that.

1. (go) We __________ to the movies once a week. We have __________ for several years. Last night we __________ to the Rialto.

2. (grow) Every summer Mrs. Ray __________ tomatoes. Over the years, she has __________ thousands. Last year she __________ 400.

3. (have) Our library __________ an annual book sale. Many times I have __________ a part in planning it. Last year we __________ $900 in sales.

4. (run) James __________ a mile a day. I have __________ with him many times. Last year he __________ a marathon and won.

5. (see) We __________ our cousins on holidays. I __________ them last Easter. Have you __________ your cousins recently?

Check your answers on page 195.

Using Irregular Verbs IV

Here are the present tense, the past tense, and the past participle of more irregular verbs.

Present	Past	Past Participle
sing(s)	sang	sung
speak(s)	spoke	spoken
steal(s)	stole	stolen
take(s)	took	taken
tell(s)	told	told
write(s)	wrote	written

In the blanks, write the correct tense of the verb in parentheses.

- (sing) Every Sunday Anzia ___sings___ in the choir. Last Christmas she ___sang___ her first solo. Since then, she has ___sung___ more solos.

1. (speak) Ms. Molinaro __________ excellent English. Until she moved to the United States, she had __________ only Spanish. She first __________ English five years ago.

2. (steal) I __________ time from work to be with my kids. Yesterday I __________ an hour for a picnic. I wish that I could have __________ more time.

3. (take) Please __________ the trash out tonight. Your sister __________ it out last time. You haven't __________ it out for several days.

4. (tell) Juan sometimes __________ jokes. Last night he __________ a good one. I was the one who had __________ it to him.

5. (write) Vonda McIntyre __________ novels. She has __________ Star Trek novels. In 2004, she __________ my favorite, *Duty, Honor, Redemption.*

Check your answers on page 195.

Forming the Passive Voice

The **passive voice** is used when the subject of the sentence receives the action. It is often used when the person who does the action is unknown or not important. The passive voice is made up of a form of the verb *be* and the past participle of a verb.

> Passive: Soap operas are watched in millions of homes.
> Active: People in millions of homes watch soap operas.

The first sentence is passive because the subject, *soap operas,* receives the action (*are watched*). The second sentence is active because the subject, *people*, does the action (*watch*). When using the passive voice, be sure to use the past participle form of the verb.

- Soap operas are (saw, seen) all over the nation.

Underline and correct the participle error in each sentence.

- Writers of soap operas are encourage (encouraged) to create wild plots.

1. Soap opera characters are face with more problems in six months than most people have in a lifetime.
2. All the following problems were see on daytime soap operas during one week.
3. Kendall of *All My Children* was rush to the hospital when she suddenly went into labor.
4. On *As the World Turns*, J.J. was kidnap.
5. A ransom was pay, but J.J. remained missing.
6. Jeremy was carry away by thugs on *Days of Our Lives.*
7. Maxie, on *General Hospital*, was ask by Cody to steal drugs.
8. Adriana was follow to the rooftop by Rex on *One Life to Life.*
9. Kevin's and Lily's apartments were rob on *The Young and the Restless.*
10. My favorite soap opera is show only as a rerun.

Check your answers on page 195.

LANGUAGE Tip

About 750,000 black bears live in the United States and Canada. Black bears live in forests. They climb trees when they need to protect themselves.

Using Participles

The past participle form of a verb may be used as an adjective. **Participles** used as adjectives describe nouns or pronouns.

- I ate a poached egg. (The egg had been poached.)

Remember that the past participle of a regular verb is formed by adding a *d* or *ed* ending to the verb. Be sure to use the correct form for the past participle of an irregular verb.

- The police returned the (stole, stolen) car to its owner.

PART A

Turn the underlined phrase into a one-word participle.

- His heart has been broken. He has a ___broken___ heart.

1. The pies have been frozen. They are ____________ pies.
2. The kitchen has been remodeled. It is a ____________ kitchen.
3. The book has been revised. It is a ____________ book.
4. The potato has been baked. It is a ____________ potato.
5. That bank account has been closed. It is a ____________ account.
6. The apple has been peeled. It is a ____________ apple.
7. The clothes have been ironed. They are ____________ clothes.

PART B

Circle the correct verb form in parentheses.

- Bears hibernate during the winter in (hided, (hidden)) dens.

1. Sometimes bears hibernate in the holes made by (falled, fallen) trees.
2. (Cover, Covered) holes protect bears from the dangers of winter.
3. Bears cannot find berries or nuts because of the (frozen, frozed) ground.
4. They keep no (stored, store) food in their dens.
5. A bear that is suddenly awakened will have an (increase, increased) heart rate.

Check your answers on page 195.

Using Fixed-Form Helpers

The helping verbs *can, could, may, might, shall, should, will,* and *must* are unusual because their forms never change. Unlike the helping verbs *have* and *be*, **fixed-form helping verbs** do not change form to agree with the subject.

- I can go. He can go.
- I have gone. He has gone too.

> **LANGUAGE Tip**
>
> *Grammar*
>
> **Helping verbs** are sometimes called **auxiliary verbs.** The word *auxiliary* means "help."

Notice that fixed-form helping verbs are followed by the main verb, not by the past participle form of the verb.

PART A

Underline the correct verb form in parentheses.

- Computer skills (can help, can helped) you in your job.

1. Thirty years ago only experts (could use, could used) computers.
2. Today the average worker (must have, must has) basic computer skills.
3. Ted (may attend, may attended) classes given by his company.
4. He (should take, should takes) advantage of the offer.
5. You (can learn, can learned) about computers too.
6. I (might try, might tried) the classes myself.
7. Another class (will start, will starts) soon.
8. I (will go, will went) if I have time.

PART B

Write a sentence for each helping verb in parentheses.

- (might) I might buy a car.

1. (can) ______________________
2. (may) ______________________
3. (should) ______________________
4. (must) ______________________

Check your answers on page 195.

Chapter 11 Review—More About Verbs

This exercise is a review of the rules you have studied in this chapter. Underline the correct verb form in parentheses.

- Most people (have used, had used) a dictionary.

1. You (can look, can looked) up word meanings in dictionaries.
2. Over the years, publishers (have printed, had printed) dictionaries of slang, foreign languages, and science.
3. A medical dictionary (might describe, might describes) a disease.
4. Have you (knew, known) anyone who worked on a dictionary?
5. The first English dictionary (was wrote, was written) by Robert Cawdrey in 1604.
6. His work (was limit, was limited) to 3,000 "hard" words.
7. More than a century later, Samuel Johnson (created, has created) a dictionary of ordinary English words.
8. By the time he was finished, Johnson (has defined, had defined) 40,000 words.
9. In 1840, Noah Webster published his (revise, revised) edition of 70,000 definitions of American English.
10. Editions of Webster's book (have become, has become) standard references in public schools.
11. Students use the dictionaries to correct (misspell, misspelled) words.
12. Until the computer was invented, editing a dictionary (has been, had been) the task of many people.
13. Now much of the work (is did, is done) by computer.

Check your answers on page 195.

Chapter 12

Test Skill

Adjectives and Adverbs

Identifying Adjectives

An **adjective** describes a noun or a pronoun by telling what kind, which one, or how many.

What kind?	I collect stoneware mugs.
Which one?	Bring me the other one.
How many?	I now have more than fifty mugs.

Underline the adjective that describes the boldface noun.

- For centuries, folk **potteries** have existed in South Korea.

1. Today this **tradition** is dying out.
2. Few **potters** now make traditional wares.
3. These people live in remote **areas** of the country.
4. The Bu Chang Myun pottery lies far off the main **road.**
5. Its three kilns fire earthenware in seven **days.**
6. Firing is the heating of the clay **pots.**
7. The kilns are huge **ovens** fueled by wood.
8. A smaller **pottery** is owned by Kim Hyun-Schick.
9. He has found a good **way** to shorten the firing time.
10. A shorter **firing** means lower costs.
11. These potteries produce roof **tiles.**
12. They also make storage **jars** for pickled vegetables.
13. Korean **potters** may also work with delicate porcelain.
14. They re-create ancient **glazes.**
15. These **people** are proud of their work.

Check your answers on page 196.

Finding Adjectives in Sentences

Adjectives often come directly before the nouns they describe.

- At times, people need legal advice.

However, adjectives can also come after the nouns (or pronouns) they describe. Adjectives that come after nouns usually follow forms of the verb *be* or other verbs that do not show action.

- His plan is legal.
- It also seems logical.

Underline the adjective that describes the boldface noun or pronoun. In the blank, write A if the adjective comes after the noun or pronoun or B if it comes before.

- A **Laws** are necessary.
- B Officials try to write good **laws**.

1. ________ **Laws** usually seem sensible.
2. ________ They help protect innocent **people**.
3. ________ But sometimes **laws** seem weird.
4. ________ Dick Hyman has written a book about strange **laws**.
5. ________ Some laws have reasonable **explanations**.
6. ________ A law in Ouray, Colorado, provides one **example**.
7. ________ **It** is illegal to hunt elk on Ouray's Main Street.
8. ________ You might think **this** is funny.
9. ________ But in mountain **towns**, elk can get in the street.
10. ________ A law in Massachusetts provides another **example**.
11. ________ Debt **collectors** cannot wear costumes on the job.
12. ________ The law prevents collectors from pretending to be police **officers**.
13. ________ My **town** has laws that seem pointless.
14. ________ Are there unusual **laws** in your town?

Check your answers on page 196.

Identifying Adverbs

An **adverb** describes a verb, an adjective, or another adverb. Adverbs tell how, how much, when, or where.

How?	Cara walked quickly down the street.
How much?	She was very upset.
When?	Then Cara felt ill.
Where?	She wanted to go home.

LANGUAGE Tip

Grammar

Sometimes groups of words are used as adverbs.

How? in a hurry

When? on my birthday

Where? near the corner

Many adverbs end in *ly*. A few common adverbs that do not end in *ly* are *almost, never, not, quite, very,* and *too*. Often an adverb comes directly after the word it describes. However, adverbs can appear anywhere in a sentence.

- Here is our new house.
- We are slowly repairing it.
- We wish we could move in immediately.

PART A

Match each adverb with the question it answers.

- __d__ here (a) How?

1. _____ immediately (b) How much?
2. _____ carefully (c) When?
3. _____ quite (d) Where?

PART B

Underline the adverb that describes the boldface word or words. The question in parentheses will help you find the adverb.

- Today only a few bison **are living** in the American West. (When?)

1. A hundred years ago, thousands of bison **roamed** there. (Where?)
2. Bison often **attack** if their calves are in danger. (When?)
3. A very **thick** coat of fur keeps bison warm in winter. (How much?)
4. They **can run** quickly even though they weigh 2,000 pounds. (How?)
5. Bison **are surviving** well in wildlife refuge parks. (How?)

Check your answers on page 196.

Forming Adjectives and Adverbs

If you want to describe a noun or a pronoun, use an adjective. If you want to describe a verb, an adjective, or an adverb, use an adverb. In many cases, you can turn an adjective into an adverb by adding an *ly* ending.

Adjective describing a noun: The fierce wind blew.
Adverb describing a verb: The wind blew fiercely.

LANGUAGE Tip

Navajo (NA vuh HOH)

The Navajo have a large reservation in the state of Arizona. Members of this Native American tribe are known for making rugs, baskets, and silver jewelry.

In the blanks, write the correct form—the adjective or the adverb—of the word in parentheses. You will use each word twice.

- (courageous) Navajo code talkers courageously helped the Marines during World War II. Because the code talkers were so courageous, they were honored by the president of the United States.

1. (secret) In 1942, the Navajo were __________ trained to send messages. Their __________ messages weren't understood by the Japanese.
2. (complete) The Navajo language was a __________ mystery to outsiders. Messages were __________ secret.
3. (perfect) Navajo was the __________ language because almost no one except the Navajo spoke this language. A trial message was sent, and it was __________ understood.
4. (frequent) The Navajo __________ made up codes for words such as "submarine." During one battle, __________ messages were needed, so code talkers didn't sleep for two days.
5. (successful) Messages could be __________ sent in seconds. The __________ project brought respect to the code talkers.

Check your answers on page 196.

Choosing Adjectives or Adverbs

Do not confuse the adjective and adverb forms of a word. In the sentence below, the adverb *really* describes the adjective *good*.

- *The Miracle Worker* is a (real, really) good play.

In the next example, the adjective *real* describes the noun *treat*.

- Watching it is a (real, really) treat.

PART A

Underline the correct form—the adjective or the adverb—in parentheses.

- A (serious, seriously) childhood illness made Helen Keller deaf and unable to speak.

1. The only sounds she made were (loud, loudly) noises.
2. She was also (complete, completely) blind.
3. Helen's parents hired a (hopeful, hopefully) young teacher.
4. Anne Sullivan worked (patient, patiently) with the child.
5. Helen (slow, slowly) learned to read and write in Braille.
6. By age 16, Helen could speak (clear, clearly) enough to go to school.
7. When she was in college, she wrote a book about her (unusual, unusually) life.
8. As an adult, Keller was (active, actively) in organizations for the blind.
9. Her accomplishments were (true, truly) impressive.
10. When she died in 1968, she was one of the most (famous, famously) women in the world.

PART B

Underline and correct the adjective or adverb error in each sentence.

beautifully
- Moshe thinks he sings beautiful.

Actually his singing is awfully. We all leave the room quick when he sings. If he sang quietly, it wouldn't be so badly. But his voice is loudly enough to hear in the next room!

Check your answers on page 196.

Making Comparisons with Adjectives

These guidelines will help you use adjectives in **comparisons.**

To compare two people or things, add an *er* ending to short adjectives (words with only one or two syllables).

- Jack may be younger than I am, but I am healthier.

The word *more* or *less* is used to compare two people or things when the adjective is long (usually three or more syllables). Sometimes two-syllable adjectives use *more* or *less* instead of an *er* ending.

- I am more athletic than Jack.
- I am less handsome than my oldest brother.

To compare three or more people or things, add an *est* ending to short adjectives.

- Of the four brothers in our family, I am the smartest.

The word *most* or *least* is used to compare three people or things when the adjective is long. A few short adjectives use *most* or *least* instead of an *er* ending.

- Of all the brothers, Jack is the least rebellious.
- Jack is also the most skilled as a musician.

Never use *more, less, most,* or *least* with an adjective ending in *er* or *est.*

- Jack is the (most tidiest, tidiest) man I know.

Underline the correct form of the adjective in parentheses.

- Rivermen are America's (more colorful, most colorful) heroes.

1. They took pride in being (tougher, toughest) than most other people.
2. They were the (less modest, least modest) of all heroes.
3. Mike Fink was the (more famous, most famous) riverman.
4. He bragged that he was the (strongest, most strongest).
5. He also claimed to be (faster, more faster) than other men.
6. Davy Crockett was said to be (less skilled, least skilled) with a rifle than Fink.

Check your answers on page 196.

Using Irregular Adjectives

Irregular adjectives change form when they are used in comparisons. The two most common irregular adjectives are *good* and *bad*.

	Comparing Two	Comparing Three or More
good	better	best
bad	worse	worst

- Woody was a better singer than Arlo.
- Martin is the worst singer I have ever heard.

Do not use the word *more* or *most* with irregular adjectives. Do not add *er* or *est* endings to irregular adjectives.

- The medicine will make him feel (better, more better).
- His cold is (worser, worse) today than it was yesterday.

PART A

In the blank, write the correct form of the word in parentheses.

- This year's company picnic was the ___best___ ever. (good)

1. Mahmud made the ______________ potato salad I have ever tasted. (good)
2. I must admit that it was even ______________ than my own. (good)
3. I was the ______________ of all the volleyball players. (bad)
4. I was even ______________ than Myra, who had a sprained wrist. (bad)

PART B

Underline and correct the adjective error in each sentence.

- *CSI* is one of the most best TV shows I've ever seen. (best)

I think it is more better than any other detective show. The most worstest TV show is *Fear Factor*. I think it is worser than *Survivor*.

Check your answers on page 196.

Making Comparisons with Adverbs

These guidelines will help you use adverbs in comparisons.

When comparing two people or things, use *more* or *less* with adverbs that end in *ly*. Use *most* or *least* with these adverbs when comparing three or more people or things.

- Sally ran <u>more quickly</u> than Randall. In fact, Sally ran the <u>most quickly</u> of all the runners.

Add an *er* ending (when comparing two people or things) or an *est* ending (when comparing three or more people or things) to adverbs that do not end in *ly*.

- Alma types <u>faster</u> than I, but Mal types <u>fastest</u> of all.

The adverb *well* is irregular. When comparing two people or things, use *better*. When comparing three or more, use *best*.

- Ruth did <u>well</u>. Alfie did <u>better</u>. Ron did the <u>best</u>.

Underline the correct form of the adverb in parentheses.

- Some people age (<u>more gracefully</u>, gracefuller) than others.

1. At age 105, Pete Lavoy plays (harder, more hard) than many people half his age.
2. Does Lavoy age (less rapid, less rapidly) than most of us?
3. Or does he just live life (more fully, fuller)?
4. Lavoy's neighbors think he must eat (less often, least often) than they do.
5. He gets around (more well, better) than you can imagine.
6. Of all his interests, he is still (more actively, most actively) involved in farming.
7. Lavoy exercises (more frequently, frequentlier) than many of his neighbors.
8. Lavoy still talks about a corn-picking contest where he did the (better, best) of all the farmers in the area.
9. The other farmers hope Lavoy continues to live (well, most well) and be healthy.

Check your answers on page 197.

Revising Double Negatives

Some words are negative in meaning. Common negatives are *no, not, never, nothing, nobody, no one,* and *none*. Words such as *hardly* and *scarcely* are also negatives.

Do not use two negatives together. This error is known as a **double negative**.

Incorrect:	The Abdullah family did not ask for no help.
Correct:	The Abdullah family did not ask for any help.

The adverb *not* can be combined with helping verbs to make contractions such as *isn't, aren't, haven't,* or *don't*. Do not use *ain't* in place of these contractions.

Incorrect:	Mrs. Abdullah ain't home.
Correct:	Mrs. Abdullah isn't home.

Circle the letter of the correctly worded sentence in each pair.

- (a) I couldn't afford to buy any milk.
  (b) I couldn't afford to buy no milk.

1. (a) We have scarcely enough money to pay the rent.
   (b) We haven't scarcely enough money to pay the rent.
2. (a) I don't know anything about budgeting money.
   (b) I don't know nothing about budgeting money.
3. (a) No one has never offered us help.
   (b) No one has ever offered us help.
4. (a) Anyway, we wouldn't accept no charity.
   (b) Anyway, we wouldn't accept any charity.
5. (a) But we can't pay none of these bills.
   (b) But we can't pay any of these bills.
6. (a) I haven't ever felt so unhappy.
   (b) I ain't ever felt so unhappy.
7. (a) I don't hardly know what to do.
   (b) I hardly know what to do.

Check your answers on page 197.

Chapter 12 Review—Adjectives and Adverbs

This exercise is a review of the rules you have studied in this chapter. Underline the correct adjective or adverb form in parentheses.

- Hurricanes are (natural, naturally) disasters.

1. Hurricanes start as (whirling, whirlingly) masses of air.
2. They are the (more, most) destructive storms on Earth.
3. Hurricane Katrina was one of the (worse, worst) U.S. storms.
4. In an (unbelievable, unbelievably) short time, one million people on the Gulf Coast lost their homes.
5. People didn't have (no, any) electricity or water.
6. Of the four states hit, Alabama was (less, least) damaged.
7. (Entire, Entirely) towns in Louisiana and Mississippi were washed away.
8. Many families found they had (almost, hardly) nothing left.
9. Survival became (more, most) important than anything else.
10. (Large, Largely) groups of people were bused to cities all around the United States.
11. Thousands had no (more better, better) place to live than a small apartment in a faraway state.
12. Many people thought relief efforts were (poor, poorly) organized.
13. The Red Cross was (bestest, best) prepared to help.
14. Volunteers worked (tireless, tirelessly).
15. The amount of money donated by private citizens was (impressive, impressively).
16. The government sent (less, least) aid than people had hoped for.
17. Recovery from such a disaster happens (slow, slowly).
18. Victims (ain't, aren't) ever going to forget Hurricane Katrina.

LANGUAGE Tip

Weather reporters name storms so they can keep track of more than one storm at a time. If a hurricane causes a great deal of damage, its name is not used again.

Check your answers on page 197.

Chapter 13

Test Skill

Sentence Structure

> **LANGUAGE Tip**
> The Otis Elevator Company is the largest elevator company in the world. There are Otis elevators in the Empire State Building and the Eiffel Tower. The next time you are in an elevator, look for the OTIS sign.

Using End Marks

A sentence should be followed by an **end mark**—a period, a question mark, or an exclamation point.

Use a period at the end of a sentence that gives information.

- The elevator is over there.

Use a question mark at the end of a sentence that asks something.

- Where are you going?

Use an exclamation point at the end of a sentence that shows strong feeling.

- We won!

Use a period at the end of a sentence that makes a request or tells someone what to do. If this sentence shows strong feeling, use an exclamation point.

- Wait for me here.
- Call the fire department!

In the blank, write the correct end mark.

- The elevator door is stuck.

1. We're trapped ___
2. Please try to stay calm ___
3. Now press the emergency button___
4. Do you know how the modern elevator was developed___
5. In 1852, Elisha Otis figured out how to make elevators safer___
6. His invention stopped elevators from falling suddenly___
7. Can you imagine tall buildings without elevators___

Check your answers on page 197.

Understanding Simple Sentences

A **simple sentence** consists of one independent clause. An **independent clause** has a subject and a predicate, and it expresses a complete thought. The **subject** is the person, place, or thing that the clause is about. The **predicate** tells what the subject does or is. The predicate always contains a verb.

- Frederick Douglass was a leader of the antislavery movement.

Subject:	Frederick Douglass
Predicate:	was a leader of the antislavery movement
Verb:	was

Draw a line between the subject and the predicate.

- Frederick Douglass/was the son of a enslaved black woman.

1. Most slave owners didn't want enslaved people to read.
2. Mrs. Auld broke the law in Maryland.
3. This slave owner taught young Douglass how to read.
4. Mr. Auld beat Douglass for learning.
5. Douglass escaped slavery in 1838.
6. He began to speak out against slavery.
7. People were inspired by Douglass's words.
8. Douglass wrote a book about his life.
9. The book is called *Life and Time of Frederick Douglass.*
10. You should read it.
11. Douglass held a government post later in his life.
12. He served as a U.S. minister and consul general to Haiti from 1889 to 1891.

Check your answers on page 197.

Understanding Compound Sentences I

A **compound sentence** is made up of two simple sentences (independent clauses) joined by a **coordinating conjunction**—*and, but, yet, so, nor, or,* or *for*. Use a comma before the coordinating conjunction in a compound sentence.

Simple Sentence:	Julio is studying.
Simple Sentence:	Toshiro is helping him.
Compound Sentence:	Julio is studying, and Toshiro is helping him.

Do not put a comma before a coordinating conjunction that is not joining independent clauses. In this example, *and* joins two predicates.

- Julio feels frustrated and is tired of reading.

Underline the coordinating conjunction. Add a comma before the conjunction when the conjunction is separating two independent clauses.

- Amelia Bloomer was a feminist writer, but she is better remembered for her unusual clothes.
- Bloomer didn't mean to set a fashion nor to become famous.

1. She supported women's rights and spoke out against slavery.
2. Bloomer disliked wide hoopskirts so she wore loose trousers under a short skirt.
3. Her clothes attracted a lot of attention for women didn't usually wear trousers in the mid-1800s.
4. Bloomer thought her clothing was practical but many people were shocked.
5. People stared rudely or laughed at her "bloomers."
6. The trouser outfit didn't catch on yet the term *bloomers* is still remembered.

Check your answers on page 197.

Understanding Compound Sentences II

There is a second way to form compound sentences. Join the two simple sentences (independent clauses) with a semicolon, a connecting word, and a comma.

Simple Sentence:	I felt ill.
Simple Sentence:	I left early.
Compound Sentence:	I felt ill; therefore, I left early.

Here are some connecting words that are commonly used in this way.

moreover	therefore	on the other hand
furthermore	as a result	however
in addition	thus	otherwise

Join each pair of sentences with a semicolon, a connecting word, and a comma.

- You must study;__otherwise,__you will not pass the test.

1. Michel was bored with his job ____________________ he wanted a position with higher pay.
2. His typing skills were good ____________________ he needed better computer skills.
3. Michel started computer classes____________________ his skill improved quickly.
4. Counselors told Michel about job openings ____________________ they taught him how to answer interviewers' questions.
5. Michel's new job is fun and pays well ____________________ Michel is glad he went back to school.
6. Sometimes people have to learn new skills ____________________ they may get stuck in dead-end jobs.

Check your answers on page 197.

Fixing Run-Ons and Comma Splices

Two common sentence errors are run-ons and comma splices.

A **run-on sentence** occurs when two sentences are joined without proper punctuation or a conjunction. A **comma splice** occurs when two sentences are joined by a comma but no conjunction.

- The electrician is late he will try to hurry.
- The electrician is late, he will try to hurry.

Here are three ways to fix run-ons and comma splices.

1. Separate the two sentences with a period.
    - The electrician is late. He will try to hurry.
2. Form a compound sentence, using a coordinating conjunction.
    - The electrician is late, but he will try to hurry.
3. Form a compound sentence with a connecting word such as *however*.
    - The electrician is late; however, he will try to hurry.

Correct the four comma splices and six run-on sentences by using the methods described above. Use each method at least once.

- Richardo bought a used computer. The owner said it worked well.

The computer worked just fine at first one day the computer would not start. Richardo thought someone at a nearby repair shop could help him he took the computer to the shop. The clerk said the computer was old they could not fix it. Richardo was frustrated, he was not going to give up. The computer was not very old, why couldn't it be repaired?

The yellow pages had a list of computer repair shops other shops were advertised in the newspaper. Richardo called two shops, his son called several others. The man at one shop said he could help, Richardo took the computer in. The repair took only a few minutes a battery needed to be replaced. Richardo's computer worked well when he took it home the repair had cost only $20.

Check your answers on page 198.

Understanding Complex Sentences I

A **complex sentence** is made up of one independent clause and one or more dependent clauses. A **dependent clause** has a subject and a predicate, but it cannot stand alone as a sentence because it is not a complete thought. Dependent clauses start with **subordinating conjunctions.**

Common Subordinating Conjunctions

after	before	until
although	if	when
as	since	where
because	so	while

Put a comma after a dependent clause that begins a sentence.

- When opportunity knocks, you should open the door.

When a dependent clause follows an independent clause, no comma is needed.

- You should open the door when opportunity knocks.

Underline the dependent clause. If the dependent clause begins the sentence, add a comma after the clause.

- When Margaret Brown bought a $4,000 ticket for a trip on the *Titanic*, she didn't think the ship would sink.
- She wanted to return to America because her grandson was sick.

1. Margaret lived in Missouri while she was growing up.
2. After Margaret married J. J. Brown he struck gold.
3. The Browns moved to Denver because they wanted a bigger house.
4. In April 1912, Margaret boarded the *Titanic* so she could return from her vacation.
5. Until the ship started sinking Margaret was reading a book.
6. She could survive only if she could get to a lifeboat.
7. Although Margaret was tired from rowing she helped as many people as she could.
8. Margaret has been known as the "unsinkable Molly Brown" since she survived her trip on the *Titanic*.

Check your answers on page 198.

Understanding Complex Sentences II

A **relative clause** is a special kind of dependent clause. It begins with a relative pronoun—*who, which,* or *that*. Relative clauses have special rules for punctuation.

1. **Nonessential** relative clauses have commas around them. The reader does not need the clause to understand the sentence, but the clause does provide extra information. Nonessential clauses begin with *which* or *who*.
   - *Happy Feet*, which is my favorite animated movie, is on DVD.
   - It is about emperor penguins, which live only in Antarctica.
   - Robin Williams, who is known for his funny voices, is the voice of both Ramon and Lovelace.

2. **Essential** relative clauses do not have commas around them. The reader needs the information in the clause to understand the sentence. Essential clauses begin with *that* or *who*.
   - The penguins that star in the movie can sing and dance.
   - I like the actress who is the voice of Gloria.

Underline each relative clause. Punctuate nonessential clauses.

- Unicorns are horned horses that exist only in fairy tales.
- Children often believe in unicorns, which are said to have magical powers.

1. Bigfoot is a huge beast that some adults believe in.

2. Reports of Bigfoot sightings which are not supported with evidence have been studied by scientists.

3. People who believe in Bigfoot try to prove its existence.

4. John Napier who worked for the Smithsonian Institution wrote a book about the creature.

5. Napier also believes in the yeti which is similar to Bigfoot.

Check your answers on page 198.

Correcting Sentence Fragments I

A **sentence fragment** is an incomplete sentence that is capitalized and punctuated as if it were a complete sentence. One common type of sentence fragment occurs when a writer capitalizes the beginning of a dependent clause and puts a period after it.

- Luis was worried. Because he lost his job.
- I wrote to Sharon Naus. Who is our insurance agent.

Correct fragments by combining them with independent clauses.

- Luis was worried because he lost his job.
- I wrote to Sharon Naus, who is our insurance agent.

Underline the sentence fragments. Then rewrite the paragraph so there are no fragments. Be sure to punctuate correctly.

- I worry about the cost of health care. Which keeps rising.

  I worry about the cost of health care, which keeps rising.

The problem is the increasing cost of insurance premiums. Which are too expensive for many people. Millions of people are suffering. Because they need medical care but do not have insurance. Every day there are children. Who do not get medical care. Although many families have medical insurance. They may not be able to afford it in the future. This problem has been recognized by political leaders such as Ted Kennedy, Hillary Clinton, and Barack Obama. Who are all members of the U.S. Senate.

Check your answers on page 198.

Correcting Sentence Fragments II

Sentence fragments also occur when writers capitalize and punctuate phrases as if they were complete sentences. A **phrase** is a group of words that may include a subject or a predicate but not both. A phrase does not state a complete thought and cannot stand alone as a complete sentence.

Here are two ways to correct a fragment that is a phrase.

1. Figure out what part of the sentence is missing—the subject, the predicate, or both. Then add the missing part.

Fragment with no predicate:	The president of the company.
Correction:	The president of the company called.
Fragment with no subject:	Looked in the phone book.
Correction:	Tim looked in the phone book.

2. Combine the phrase with a complete sentence.

Sentence and a fragment:	My house is on Capitol Drive. In Milwaukee.
Correction:	My house is on Capitol Drive in Milwaukee.

Underline the sentence fragments. Then rewrite the paragraph so there are no fragments. Be sure to punctuate correctly.

- Ben Franklin was worried. About fires in Philadelphia.

  Ben Franklin was worried about fires in Philadelphia.

Many people tried to help whenever there was a fire. In the city. But they did not have equipment. Or know how to fight fires. In 1735 Franklin sent a letter. To his own newspaper. He suggested that the same group of men. Always travel with a fire engine. By practicing, they would learn. How to fight fires. They could also. Hold meetings to discuss fire prevention. Franklin's ideas were the beginning. Of modern fire departments.

Check your answers on page 198.

Chapter 13 Review—Sentence Structure

This exercise is a review of the rules you have studied in this chapter. Circle the letter of the correct sentence in each pair.

LANGUAGE Tip

Iroquois (IR uh KWOY)

The Iroquois lived in the state of New York. They were known for decorating their clothing with fancy beadwork.

- (a) The Iroquois tribes united before America existed.
  (b) The Iroquois tribes united, before America existed.

1. (a) We read and talked about the tribes in school.
   (b) We read, and talked about the tribes in school.
2. (a) Five tribes created the system. That was called the League of Five Nations.
   (b) Five tribes created the system that was called the League of Five Nations.
3. (a) After the league was formed, the tribes stopped fighting one another.
   (b) After the league was formed the tribes stopped fighting one another.
4. (a) Their council, which consisted of 50 chiefs, handled business between the tribes.
   (b) Their council which consisted of 50 chiefs handled business between the tribes.
5. (a) The league had unwritten laws. Based on tribal needs.
   (b) The league had unwritten laws based on tribal needs.
6. (a) The tribes worked together each tribe governed itself.
   (b) The tribes worked together; however, each tribe governed itself.
7. (a) Women had power, for they appointed the chiefs.
   (b) Women had power, they appointed the chiefs.
8. (a) Did you know that Ben Franklin studied this system!
   (b) Did you know that Ben Franklin studied this system?
9. (a) Franklin, who helped plan the U.S. government, borrowed ideas from the Iroquois.
   (b) Franklin who helped plan the U.S. government borrowed ideas from the Iroquois.

Check your answers on page 198.

Posttest

This posttest will give you a chance to see how much you remember about what you have studied. Take the test without looking in the book for help or answers.

The test has been divided into two sections. The first section is a test of your writing ability. It asks you to write a short essay. The second section is a test of your overall knowledge of the grammar, mechanics, and usage rules covered in this book.

Once you complete the test, check your answers on pages 179–181. Then fill out the Posttest Evaluation Chart on page 178. The chart will tell you which sections of the book you might want to review.

Section I: Writing

Carefully read the assignments below. Pick *one* of these assignments to write about. Then use the writing process to write an essay about the topic of your choice. Begin by prewriting—planning what you want to say. Then write a first draft. Finally, revise and edit your draft.

ASSIGNMENT A: *Narrative*

On a piece of paper, write a narrative (a story about an event in your life). You can write about one of the following events or about another event of your choice.

- my first date
- my best (or worst) experience in school
- the craziest (or happiest) day of my life

Use time order to organize your narrative. End your narrative with a main-idea sentence that states the point of your story.

ASSIGNMENT B: *Descriptive*

On a piece of paper, write a description (an essay that describes a person, place, or thing). You can write about one of the following topics or about another topic of your choice.

- a spring event in a high school gym on a hot day
- the waiting room at a doctor's (or dentist's) office
- the most beautiful (or ugliest) place you have even been

Help readers picture what you are describing. Use details that appeal to one of more of the five senses—seeing, hearing, smelling, touching, and tasting. Use space order to organize your description.

ASSIGNMENT C: Example

On a piece of paper, write an essay in which you support a main idea with examples. You can write about one of the following topics or about another topic of your choice.

- great (or terrible) bosses
- the annoying habits of coworkers
- ways to entertain kids on a rainy day

Be sure that your essay begins with a clear statement of the main idea. Use order of importance to organize your examples. Restate your main idea in the conclusion.

Section II: Grammar, Mechanics, and Usage

PART A: Nouns

This part tests your knowledge of common and proper nouns, singular and plural nouns, and possessive nouns. Underline and correct the error in each sentence.

- In 2003, America's space program had another disaster.

1. The space shuttle *Columbia* exploded on saturday, February 1.
2. It happened over Texas in Winter.
3. Six U.S. astronaut and one Israeli astronaut had been on a 16-day trip.
4. Family members were waiting at Kennedy space Center for the shuttle to land.
5. People in citys all across the United States were watching TV so they could see the shuttle land.
6. The shuttle broke into pieces just before it was supposed to land in florida.
7. Later many scientists studied what had happened and why the heros were lost.
8. The scientists report said that a piece of foam had been damaged when the shuttle lifted off.
9. Scientists hope this information will prevent more tragedys.
10. Men's and womens' faith in the space program was shaken by the disaster.
11. Everyone hopes that no more lifes will be lost.
12. The shuttles crew was honored when a Colorado mountain was named Columbia Point.

PART B: Verbs

This part tests your knowledge of verb tenses, verb forms, and subject-verb agreement. Underline the correct form of the verb in parentheses.

- Can a mountain (become, becomes) a sculpture?

1. Mount Rushmore (stand, stands) in the Black Hills of South Dakota.
2. (Do, Does) you know about this monument?
3. Carvings of four presidential faces (exist, exists) in stone.
4. The giant sculpture (are, is) a famous landmark.
5. The carving of the monument (start, started) in 1927.
6. The project (took, takes) 14 years to finish.
7. The site (was chose, was chosen) by the artist, John Borglum.
8. He (wanted, has wanted) to use the fine granite found in this mountain.
9. Borglum made sure that he could (carve, carved) faces that would look real.
10. He (make, made) a plaster cast to use as a model of the faces.
11. After workers (have, had) drilled holes in the rock, dynamite was inserted.
12. By the end of the project, workers (had blew, had blown) away more than 450,000 tons of rock.
13. Many people (went, gone) to watch the workers carving the stone.
14. President Roosevelt (saw, seen) the incomplete monument in 1936.
15. Work (was, were) still progressing when the artist died.
16. The (finish, finished) sculpture was unveiled by Borglum's son.
17. Over the years, the mountain (has became, has become) famous.
18. It will (continue, continued) to attract tourists.

PART C: Pronouns, Adjectives, and Adverbs

This part tests your knowledge of pronoun, adjective, and adverb forms and usage. Underline the correct form of the pronoun, adjective, or adverb in parentheses.

- Rockabilly music became (popular, popularly) in the 1950s.

1. Johnny Cash was one of the (best, bestest) performers.
2. Sun Records gave (he, him), Elvis Presley, and Jerry Lee Lewis their start.
3. Their music caught on (quick, quickly) with young people.
4. Cash and two friends formed (their, there) own band.
5. They called (themselfs, themselves) Johnny Cash and the Tennessee Two.
6. Success did not come (easy, easily) for the group.
7. Singing for a living was (harder, hardest) than they expected.
8. At first, the band was paid hardly (nothing, anything).
9. Cash says (them, those) early days were rough.
10. With success, his days seemed even (longer, more longer).
11. The (more hurried, hurrieder) his life got, the more pep pills he took.
12. The singer's life was more stressful than (mine, mine's).
13. Drug abuse caused problems between (he, him) and his wife.
14. It took a (terrible, terribly) accident to make Cash give up the pills.
15. Later (he, him) and his wife won a Grammy.

PART D: Sentence Structure

This part tests your knowledge of writing and punctuating various types of sentences. Each sentence has an underlined error. Circle the letter of the correct way to revise the error.

- What is a "wrap-around" artist.

  (a) artist? (b) artist!

1. Christo Javacheff is an artist, who creates his art by wrapping large objects.

   (a) artist. Who (b) artist who

2. In Paris, Christo covered the Pont-Neuf bridge. With huge sheets of yellow cloth.

   (a) bridge with (b) bridge. Using

3. What an amazing sight that must have been.

   (a) been! (b) been?

4. Millions of people came to see the bridge, thousands of them left with a piece of cloth.

   (a) bridge thousands (b) bridge, and thousands

5. **Christo also "wrapped" some small islands in Florida they looked like tropical flowers when viewed from the air.**

   (a) Florida, they (b) Florida. They

6. **The artist takes this approach; because, he wants to make people aware of** what is around them.

   (a) approach because (b) approach. Because

7. Christo's huge works are temporary. Which has led to criticism from the art world.

   (a) temporary which (b) temporary, which

8. I can understand their point however I like Christo's work.

   (a) point; however, (b) point however,

Check your answers on pages 179–181.

Posttest Evaluation Chart

Use the Postttest Answer Key on pages 179–181 to check your answers. Next, find the number of each question you missed in Section II of the Posttest. Circle that number in the Item Numbers column of this chart. Then look at the Review Pages column to see which pages you need to review.

Grammar, Mechanics, and Usage	Item Numbers	Review Pages	Number Correct
Part A: Nouns			
Capitalization	1, 2, 4, 6	114–115	
Plurals	3, 5, 7, 9, 11	116–118	
Possessives	8, 10, 12	119–121	
Part B: Verbs			
Tense and Form	5, 6, 7, 8, 9, 10, 11, 12, 13, 14, 16, 17, 18	138–141, 143–151	
Agreement	1, 2, 3, 4, 15	134–137	
Part C: Pronouns, Adjectives, and Adverbs			
Adjective Form and Use	1, 7, 10, 11, 14	157–159	
Adverb Form and Use	3, 6	157	
Subject/Object Pronouns	2, 13, 15	124–126	
Possessive Pronouns	4, 12	128–129	
Reflexive Pronouns	5	130	
Demonstrative Pronouns	9	131	
Double Negatives	8	161	
Part D: Sentence Structure			
Sentence Types	3	163	
Compound Sentences	8	165–166	
Complex Sentences	1, 6	168–169	
Sentence Fragments	2, 7	170–171	
Run-Ons	5	167	
Comma Splices	4	167	

Posttest Answer Key

Section I: Writing, pages 173–174

Evaluate your essay by answering the questions on the Evaluation Checklist below. If possible, have a teacher, classmate, family member, or friend also evaluate your work. Then use the evaluations to revise your essay. If you need help revising, review the appropriate sections of the book.

Evaluation Checklist

Yes	No	
❑	❑	1. Does the essay have an introductory paragraph?
❑	❑	2. Is the main idea clearly stated in the introduction? (If your essay is a narrative, see Question 8.)
❑	❑	3. Does the body contain at least one paragraph?
❑	❑	4. Is the body developed with enough details to explain the main idea clearly?
❑	❑	5. Do all the details in the body support the main idea?
❑	❑	6. Are the details in the body logically organized?
❑	❑	7. Is there a paragraph of conclusion?
❑	❑	8. Does the conclusion restate the main idea? (If the essay is a narrative, does the conclusion state the main idea?)
❑	❑	9. Are there any sentences or ideas that aren't clear?
❑	❑	10. Are there errors in grammar, mechanics, or usage?

Section II: Grammar, Mechanics, and Usage

Part A: Nouns, page 174

1. **Saturday**—Capitalize the names of days of the week.
2. **winter**—Do not capitalize names of seasons.
3. **astronauts**—The clue word *six* tells you that *astronauts* should be plural.
4. **Space**—*Space* is capitalized because it is part of the name Kennedy Space Center.
5. **cities**—The plural of nouns that end in a consonant and a *y* is formed by changing the *y* to an *i* and adding *es*.
6. **Florida**—Capitalize the names of specific places.
7. **heroes**—Singular nouns ending in a consonant and an *o* form the plural with an *es* ending.
8. **scientists'**—The report belongs to the scientists. Regular plural nouns form the possessive with an apostrophe after the final *s* (*s'*)
9. **tragedies**—The plural of nouns that end in a consonant and a *y* is formed by changing the *y* to an *i* and adding *es*.

10. **women's**—Irregular nouns form the plural possessive with an apostrophe and an *s* (*'s*).
11. **lives**—for many nouns that end in *fe*, the plural is formed by changing the *f* to a *v* and adding *es*.
12. **shuttle's**—The crew belongs to the shuttle. Singular nouns form the possessive with an apostrophe and an *s* ('s).

Part B: Verbs, page 175

1. **stands**—The subject, *Mount Rushmore*, is singular.
2. **Do**—*Do* agrees with the subject, *you*.
3. **exist**—The subject, *carvings*, is plural.
4. **is**—The subject, *sculpture*, is third-person singular.
5. **started**—The action began and ended in the past.
6. **took**—The past tense of the irregular verb *take* is *took*.
7. **was chosen**—The past participle form of the irregular verb *choose* is *chosen*.
8. **wanted**—The action began and ended in the past.
9. **carve**—Main verbs do not change form when used with a fixed-form helping verb such as *could*.
10. **made**—The action began and ended in the past.
11. **had**—The past perfect shows that one action (drilling) occurred before another (inserting dynamite).
12. **had blown**—The past participle of the irregular verb *blow* is *blown*.
13. **went**—The past tense of the irregular verb *go* is *went*.
14. **saw**—The past tense of the irregular verb *see* is *saw*.
15. **was**—*Was* agrees with the singular subject, *work*.
16. **finished**—The past participle of the verb is used as an adjective to describe a noun.
17. **has become**—The past participle of the irregular verb *become* is *become*.
18. **continue**—Main verbs do not change form when used with *will* to tell about a future action.

Part C: Pronouns, Adjectives, and Adverbs, page 176

1. **best**—When comparing three or more people or things, *best* is the correct form of the adjective *good*.
2. **him**—The pronoun is the indirect object.
3. **quickly**—The adverb describes the verb phrase *caught on*. It answers the question *when?*
4. **their**—The possessive pronoun is needed to show that the band belonged to Cash and his friends.

5. **themselves**—Plural reflexive pronouns end in *selves.*
6. **easily**—The adverb describes the verb *come.* It answers the question *how?*
7. **harder**—Use an *er* ending on short adjectives when comparing two things.
8. **anything**—The sentence already contains the negative *hardly.* Adding a second negative would create a double negative.
9. **those**—The sentence calls for a demonstrative pronoun, not an object pronoun.
10. **longer**—When making a comparison, do not use both an *er* ending and the word *more.*
11. **more hurried**—Use the word *more* (not an *er* ending) with the two-syllable adjective *hurried.*
12. **mine**—*Mine* doesn't end in *'s.* None of the personal pronouns are spelled with an apostrophe.
13. **him**—The pronoun is the object of the proposition *between.*
14. **terrible**—The adjective describes the noun *accident.*
15. **he**—*He* is a subject pronoun. It is used here as part of a compound subject.

Part D: Sentence Structure, pages 176–177

1. **(b)** The original sentence is punctuated incorrectly. Choice *b* is correct because the relative clause is essential. Choice *a* creates a sentence fragment.
2. **(a)** The original sentence contains a fragment. Choice *a* correctly joins the phrase to the sentence. Choice *b* creates another fragment.
3. **(a)** The original sentence has the wrong end mark. The exclamation point in Choice *a* shows that the sentence should be read with emotion. Choice *b* incorrectly uses a question mark.
4. **(b)** The original sentence is a comma splice. Choice *b* correctly joins the independent clauses in a compound sentence. Choice *a* is a run-on sentence.
5. **(b)** The original sentence is a run-on. Choice *b* correctly separates the two independent clauses. Choice *a* creates a comma splice.
6. **(a)** The original sentence is incorrectly punctuated. Choice *a* correctly omits the punctuation at the beginning of the dependent clause. Choice *b* creates a sentence fragment.
7. **(b)** The original sentence contains a fragment. Choice *b* correctly joins the relative clause to the independent clause. Choice *a* incorrectly omits the comma before the clause.
8. **(a)** The original sentence needs punctuation. Choice *a* is correctly punctuated. Choice *b* incorrectly omits the semicolon before the connecting word *however.*

Answer Key

Part I: Writing

Chapter 1: The Essay

Exercise 1, page 5

PART A
You can find job openings in a number of ways.

PART B
a

Exercise 2, page 7

PART A
(a) two bedrooms
(b) a big basement
(c) a fireplace in the living room

PART B
b

Exercise 3, page 9

PART A
My world seemed to turn upside down the day LaTise asked for a divorce.

PART B
b

Exercise 4, pages 12–13

PART A
Main idea: As a result of working with them, I have learned what it takes to be a good boss.
Main supporting detail, paragraph 1 of body: First of all, a good boss is fair.
Main supporting detail, paragraph 2 of body: A good boss does not overload employees with work.
Main supporting detail, paragraph 3 of body: Finally, a good boss knows how to motivate people.
Restatement of main idea in conclusion: In short, a good boss is fair, reasonable, and motivating.

PART B
Supporting details and paragraphs will vary.

Chapter 2: The Writing Process

Exercise 1, page 17
Answers will vary.

Exercise 2, page 18
Answers will vary.

Exercise 3, page 19
Answers will vary.

Exercise 4, page 21
Answers will vary.

Exercise 5, page 23

PART A
Sentences will vary. Use these main-idea sentences as a guideline.

1. Here are some ways to cope when you are trying to quit smoking.
2. After my kids cook, the kitchen is a mess.
3. Everything went wrong the day that I graduated.

PART B
Sentences will vary. If possible, have someone else read your main-idea sentence to make sure that it is clear.

Exercise 6, page 25

PART A
1. **Group A: Good Points**
   (a) could come and go as I please
   (b) would feel good to be on my own
   (c) would have my own bedroom
   (d) could play music whenever I want
   Group B: Bad Points
   (a) will cost a lot
   (b) might be kind of lonely
   (c) hate to cook and clean

2.

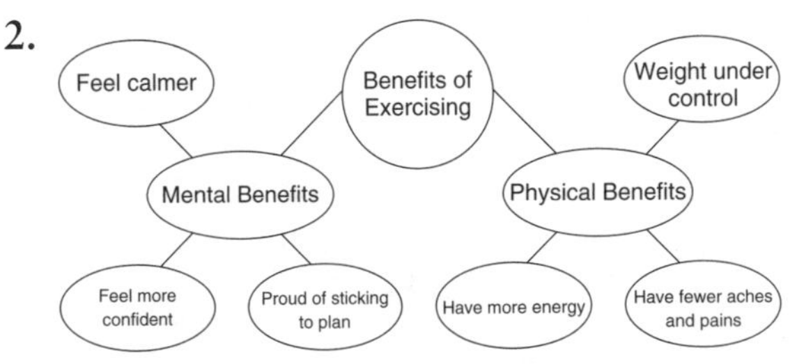

PART B

Answers will vary.

Exercise 7, page 27

Answers will vary.

Exercise 8, page 29

PART A

Answers may vary. Use these answers as a guideline.

1. No—Although there is an opening paragraph, it doesn't introduce the main point of the essay.
2. No—The introduction does not contain a main-idea sentence. (The first sentence of paragraph 2 would make a good main-idea sentence.)
3. Yes
4. Yes—The details support the main idea "I do the work of many people."
5. Yes
6. Yes
7. No
8. No
9. Yes

PART B

Answers will vary.

Take It Off! page 29

Take It Off!

Are you tired of being overweight? Would you like to look and feel better? Here are some ways to lose those extra pounds.

Begin by building good eating habits. Drink at least five glasses of water a day. Water will help cut your appetite. In addition, stay away from sugary and fatty foods. Instead, eat foods that are high in complex carbohydrates, such as potatoes or pasta.

It's also important to develop good mental habits. Each week set a realistic weight-loss goal. For example, say you will try to lose one pound. The goal will give you something specific to aim for. When you're tempted to overeat, talk yourself out of it. Picture the thin person inside yourself just waiting to get out.

You should also try to exercise each day. Walk instead of driving. Climb the stairs instead of using the elevator.

Losing weight is not easy. But you can do it if you want to and you know how. When you follow the methods in this essay, you, too, will lose weight.

Editing Exercise: Nouns, page 30

If you miss a correction, you may need to review a point of grammar. In parentheses at the end of each sentence is the number of the page where you can find an explanation of the grammar point.

Dear Reba,

I received your letter in this morning's mail (page 119). It certainly brightened a chilly Monday (page 115). It's always great to hear from my favorite aunt (page 114).

We've had an unusually cold fall this year (page 115). An early September frost took us by surprise (page 115). Most people's gardens were ruined (page 121). You should have seen my poor tomatoes (page 117)! On the other hand, the leaves are especially colorful this year (page 117).

Bo and Nedra are really looking forward to Halloween (page 115). Kids' costumes were on sale, so I bought new ghost outfits (page 120). This year we're going trick-or-treating with a few other families (page 117). It will be easier on me and more fun for the children (page 118).

It's getting late and I have to pack tomorrow's lunches, so I'll sign off for now (page 117).

Chapter 3: Describing

Exercise 1, page 33

1. b
2. b
3. a

Exercise 2, page 35
Answers will vary.

Exercise 3, page 37
1. from outside to inside
2. from far away to close up
3. from left to right

Check Your Understanding, page 40

PART A
1. a
2. a
3. b
4. a

PART B
Answers will vary. Use these answers as a guideline.

1. large orange-and-yellow shade trees, large house, friendly looking carved pumpkin, oriental rug, white quilt
2. crunchy dry leaves, door opening and slamming closed
3. apples and spices, fragrant soaps, coffee brewing
4. freshly squeezed orange juice, hot coffee, a fruit cup filled with sweet pineapple chunks, halved grapes, and juicy melon slices, pancakes covered with sliced apples and swimming in maple syrup
5. soft terry-cloth robe, warm quilt

Revision Warm-Up, page 45
Answers may vary. Use these answers as a guideline.

1. No—Although there's an opening paragraph, it doesn't introduce the essay.
2. No
3. Yes
4. No—Because there is not an overall impression.
5. No—There are a number of descriptive details, but the details do not add up to an overall impression. In addition, a few details are off the topic. Note, for example, the second sentence of paragraph 2.
6. Yes—In general, the details are arranged in order from close up to far away.
7. No—The paragraph at the end doesn't "wrap up" the essay.
8. No
9. No—Some sentences in paragraph 2 are confusing. Note, for example, the sentence "It rises from another."

Editing Exercise: Pronouns, page 46
If you miss a correction, you may need to review a point of grammar. In parentheses at the end of each sentence is the number of the page where you can find an explanation of the grammar point.

Dear Linn,

It's too bad you couldn't make it to our New Year's Eve party (page 128). Glenn and I missed having you (page 127).

About twenty of our friends showed up. As usual, the Nielands brought their kids (page 128). I usually love children, but the Nieland kids are so loud! They gave Glenn and me a headache (page 127). The Smiths sort of invited themselves (page 130). However, we didn't really mind. We enjoyed having them.

We decorated the living room with the silver streamers and balloons that you gave to us (page 126). Glenn and I put the long table on the right side of the living room (page 127). It was loaded with all kinds of food. Everyone loved Glenn's version of potato salad. Mine was less popular (page 129). However, those pizza puffs I made were gobbled up fast (page 131).

We're already beginning to plan next year's party, and we hope you can come. Put it on your calendar now!

Love, Juanaita

Chapter 4: Narrating

Exercise 1, page 49

PART A
1. As I hugged my wife and kids, I thought about what really matters to me.
2. We would prove that people working together can get rid of gangs.

PART B
b

Exercise 2, page 51

PART A

1. a
2. c
3. b

PART B

1. person against self
2. person against nature
3. person against person

Exercise 3, page 53

1. 4, 3, 1, 2, 5
2. 5, 1, 4, 3, 2
3. 3, 4, 2, 1
4. 5, 1, 3, 2, 4

Check Your Understanding, page 56

PART A

1. c
2. b
3. 4, 3, 5, 2, 1

PART B

Answers may vary. Use these answers as a guideline.

1. When the narrator is in the air and realizes that the pool is nearly empty, he figures out that kids are not supposed to be in the water. He has broken a rule and now he thinks he has a big problem.
2. I think that he is more confident and that he starts to enjoy his friends more because he is less worried about making mistakes.

Revision Warm-Up, page 61

Revisions of descriptive details and the main-idea sentence may vary. Use these revisions as a guideline.

Sky High

Last month, I found myself in a place I had never been before. I was high over my hometown in a small plane piloted by my friend Carlos. ~~Carlos and I went to grade school together.~~ I was terrified. My heart was pounding loudly in my ears, and I had closed my eyes so tightly that my forehead hurt. How did I get myself into this? I wondered.

Actually, I knew very well. My fear of flying was keeping me from getting a promotion. I was trying to overcome my fear.

"Are you OK?" Carlos asked. "I guess so," was all I could say. I was so scared that I was having trouble talking. Would I faint? I took a deep breath. Then I pictured myself on the ground, victorious. The thought made me relax. Slowly I opened one eye, then the other. I looked out the window and saw the most amazing sights. <u>I saw the whole community in miniature. My town seemed to be the size of a Monopoly game board. The houses and stores looked like pieces of the game.</u> To my surprise, I began to enjoy myself.

In no time at all, Carlos, said, "We're landing." As I left the plane, my knees were wobbly but my head was clear. <u>It was one of my proudest moments. I had overcome my fear!</u>

Editing Exercise: Verbs, page 62

If you miss a correction, you may need to review a point of grammar. In parentheses at the end of each sentence is the number of the page where you can find an explanation of the grammar point.

Back to School

I was really nervous about going back to school. My husband and kids <u>were</u> all for it (page 139). But I wasn't so sure. I <u>hated</u> school when I was a teenager (page 138). Would I hate it now? I was also afraid that I was too old for school.

Then I <u>ran</u> into an old friend (page 139). She said that she <u>was</u> taking high school classes through the library (page 141). She said that going to school was fun. She also said that age <u>doesn't</u> matter (page 136).

Now my friend and I go to class two mornings a week. I am doing very well. I love school. My husband <u>says</u> he is proud of me (page 135). My kids <u>are</u> proud too (page 136). I never thought I could do so well.

Chapter 5: Explaining How

Exercise 1, page 65

Main-idea sentence: Here are the steps that a right-handed bowler should take.
Sentence that states a benefit: If you follow them, you'll improve your chance of bowling a strike.

Exercise 2, page 67

PART A

To make a California sandwich, take two pieces of wheat bread. Spread one piece of bread with a teaspoon of mayonnaise. Then put a slice of Colby cheese on top of the mayonnaise. Layer lettuce, bean sprouts, and tomato on top of the cheese. Cover the sandwich with the second piece of bread and cut the sandwich in half.

PART B

Paragraphs will vary. Use this paragraph as a guideline.

Push the power button. Wait for the phone to turn on. Press the buttons of the telephone number. Then press send. Wait for someone to answer.

PART C

Definitions will vary. Use these definitions as guidelines.

basting a hem—holding a hem in place temporarily by sewing it with large running stitches
bleeding the brakes—making sure that excess air has been removed from a car's break lining
snapping a football—passing or handing the ball from the center to another team member in order to begin a play
choking a guitar string—pulling a guitar string upward to raise a note a half tone or pulling it downward to lower the note a half tone
creaming butter and sugar—beating the mixture until it is light and fluffy

Exercise 3, page 69

3, 1, 2, 6, 5, 4, 7

Paragraphs will vary. Use this paragraph as a guideline.

To go grocery shopping, first make a list of what you need. Then go to the store and get a shopping cart. Go up and down the aisles, selecting the food on your list. Next, empty your cart at the checkout and pay the cashier. Finally, take your food home.

Check Your Understanding, page 72

1. b
2. a
3. 4, 6, 2, 3, 5, 1
4. a
5. first, next, third, then, finally, now

Revision Warm-Up, page 77

Sit Up!

Exercise is important. Avoiding injury is just as important. Sit-ups can keep you fit, but you must be careful to do them properly.

It is important to start out in the correct position. Lie on your back with your knees up and bent. Keep your feet on the floor, about shoulder distance apart. Clasp your hands and rest them on the back of your neck.

Now pull in your lower "tummy" muscles. At the same time, push your lower back into the floor. Your head and shoulders should naturally rise from the floor. As you rise, breathe out. Be sure to keep your head and elbows back and look toward the ceiling. Hold this position. Then relax and lower your upper body. As you lower your body, breathe in.

If you follow these steps, you will do sit-ups correctly. Soon you will have a firmer and more attractive tummy.

Editing Exercise: Verbs, page 78

If you miss a correction, you may need to review a point of grammar. In parentheses at the end of each sentence is the number of the page where you can find an explanation of the grammar point.

Two Different People

My ex-girlfriend and I saw eye to eye on very few things (page 147). One of the many things we could not agree on was movies (page 151). She liked action movies—the kind in which the bad guys are killed off by a hero (page 149). She was not happy unless a car or two and maybe a building were blown up (page 145). I have always hated violent movies (page 143). I like well-written, upbeat stories about people overcoming their problems (page 150).

One Saturday night, our differences came to a head (page 146). We had just finished dinner and were arguing about what movie to see (page 144). She had been wanting to see an Arnold Schwarzenegger movie, but I wanted to see a movie about baseball (page 147). As we argued, each of us grew more stubborn (page 147).

Finally we did the only thing we could do (page 146). We went to the same theater but not to the same movie (page 147). That very evening, we broke off our relationship (page 145). We haven't spoken to each other since then (page 148). I should have known better than to date someone whose taste was so different from mine (page 147).

Chapter 6: Giving Examples

Exercise 1, page 81

Our kids see too much violence on TV.

Exercise 2, page 83

1. Mexican food is becoming more and more popular.
    - Salsa now outsells ketchup.
    - There are more than 50 Mexican restaurants in the city.
    - Tortilla chips and salsa seem to be served at every party.
2. There is a national park for you, no matter what kind of landscape you like.
    - There is the deep and vast Grand Canyon.
    - There are the high, snowcapped Rocky Mountains.
    - **There is the huge, watery Everglades swamp.**
3. Living in a country where you do not speak the language is difficult.
    - Store clerks are impatient when they cannot understand you.
    - You cannot understand what people are saying on TV shows.
    - You cannot ask for directions.

Exercise 3, page 85

b

Check Your Understanding, page 88

PART A

1. b
2. 2, 5, 9, 7, 3, 8, 6, 4
3. a

PART B

1. Answers will vary.
2. Life without the Internet has become unthinkable.

Revision Warm-Up, page 93

Revisions will vary. Use these revisions as a guideline.

Bad Drivers

Every time I drive, I cannot help noticing that drivers are getting worse and worse. I am surprised that the accident rate is not higher than it is.

Too many people just don't pay attention to their driving. When they make a turn, they forget to use their turn signals. They are so busy changing the station on the radio or talking on their cell phones that they don't seem to notice the light has changed. They also run stop signs too often.

Worse yet, many people drive much too fast. I see tailgaters every time I drive on the highway. They are in such a hurry that they don't keep a safe distance from the other drivers. Speeding drivers have also made the side streets dangerous. The street I live on used to be quiet, but speeding cars have made it unsafe. The speeders just don't care about the kids playing near the street. Will it take a tragedy to make these drivers slow down?

I wish that our police department would do a better job of stopping and ticketing bad drivers. It is time we made our streets and highways safe again.

Editing Exercise: Adjectives and Adverbs, page 94

If you miss a correction, you may need to review a point of grammar. In parentheses at the end of each sentence is the number of the page where you can find an explanation of the grammar point.

Picky Pet

My cat, Murphy, is the pickiest eater in the world (page 158). I have given her every brand of cat food on the market, but she does not like any of them (page 161). Each time I give her a new brand, she acts as if it is the worst food she has ever eaten (page 159). Yesterday I finally decided to do something to make her less fussy (page 158). I decided I would not give her anything to eat until she had cleaned up her plate (page 161).

Last night she began to meow pitifully (page 157). She had not touched the food I had given her, and the food looked terrible (page 157). It had been sitting so long that it was completely dry (page 157). She continued to meow sadly, but I pretended to ignore her (page 157).

Suddenly I heard a loud noise in the kitchen (page 157). I quickly ran to see what had happened (page 157). Murphy had flipped her bowl over and was making the worst mess I had ever seen (page 159). The cat meowed loudly and happily as I opened a can of tuna (page 157). I hated to give in, but I figured it was better than putting up with her tantrums (page 159).

Chapter 7: Comparing and Contrasting

Exercise 1, page 97

1. b
2. a

Exercise 2, page 99

Answers will vary. Use these answers as a guideline.

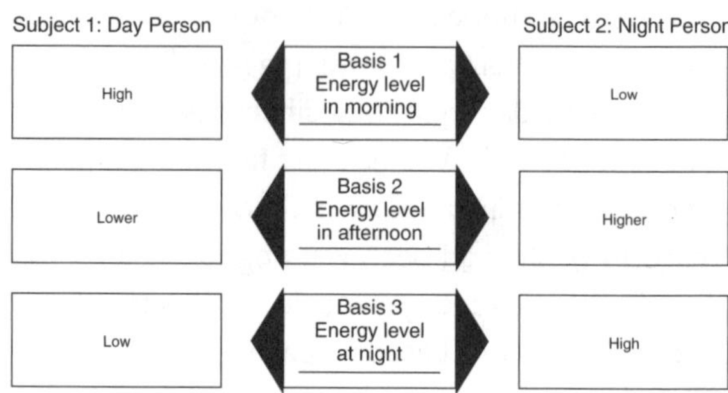

Exercise 3, page 101

1. b
2. a

Check Your Understanding, page 104

PART A

1. a
2. size, sleeping habits, eating habits, attachment to humans, ability to defend against burglars, style of movement
3. b

PART B

1. Cats and dogs are different, but they are both fun.
2. Answers will vary.

Revision Warm-Up, page 109

Revisions will vary. Use these revisions as a guideline.

Yesterday and Today

I'm more mature now than when I was at sixteen. Recently I had my twenty-sixth birthday. As I do on all my birthdays, I looked back on my past. The last ten years have been tough. However, I feel that my life is finally going in the right direction.

When I was sixteen, I was a know-it-all. My parents begged me to stay in school, but I ignored them. They seemed so hopelessly out of touch with the world and my life. Now that I am twenty-six, I know my parents were right. As a dropout, I have not been able to get very good jobs. To better myself, I have gone back to school. I know I have a lot to learn.

At sixteen, I had very little focus in life. In fact, I had only two goals. I wanted to get a job so I could buy a nice car and fancy clothes. I also wanted to be friends with the "right" people. In contrast, my goals today are very different. I don't care about fancy clothes or cars. I spend more time with family than with friends. Now I want to get a good education and find a good job.

I still have a long way to go to reach my goals. But I know I will achieve them. I like myself better today than I ever have, and I believe my life is on the right track.

Editing Exercise: Sentence Structure, page 110

If you miss a correction, you may need to review a point of grammar. In parentheses at the end of each sentence is the number of the page where you can find an explanation of the grammar point.

On My Own

Should I get my own apartment? (page 163) That was the question I kept asking myself. Finally I decided to go ahead, and I rented my own place (page 165). Although it is expensive being on my own, it is well worth it (page 168).

I love the freedom of being independent. I answer to no one. (page 167) I come and go as I please. If I come in at 3 o'clock in the morning, there is no one yelling at me, asking me where I have been (page 170).

I also enjoy my new-found privacy. When I lived at home, my little brother was always poking his nose in my business. I could not talk on the phone to my friends without my little brother listening in on our calls (page 171). Now my life is much better. (page 167) I am able to keep private things private.

It is expensive to be on my own; however, I don't mind paying the price (page 166). I guess I am just one of those people who are better off being on their own (page 170).

Part II: Grammar

Chapter 8: Nouns

Identifying Nouns, page 113

PART A

1. William Cody, Iowa
2. boy, Cody, rider, Pony Express
3. Cody, wife, children
4. Buffalo Bill, Wild West Show
5. people, horses, show, parade
6. actors, contest, stagecoach
7. People, West, railroads, land
8. show, world, Cody, Pope
9. Cody, Golden, Colorado

PART B

Answers will vary.

Capitalizing Nouns I, page 114

1. New Orleans
2. Luis, Tulane University
3. Lake Pontchartrain
4. Lee, Bourbon Street
5. French Quarter
6. Jackson Square
7. Uncle Jerome
8. Jerome, Congresswoman Jones
9. Hilton Hotel
10. Buddy Guy
11. Preservation Hall
12. Paris Road
13. Jana, Mississippi River
14. Hurricane Katrina

Capitalizing Nouns II, page 115

PART A

1. Thanksgiving, Monday
2. Friday, Halloween
3. Saturday, Valentine's Day, Friday
4. New Year's Eve, May
5. January
6. Presidents' Day
7. Christmas
8. December

PART B

Answers will vary.

Identifying Plural Nouns, page 116

PART A

1. S
2. P
3. S
4. P
5. P

PART B

Hsu put out a stack of <u>napkins</u> for the whole family. Then Mr. Nurachi brought in several <u>bowls</u> of beans. Hsu's mother placed a pair of <u>chopsticks</u> by each plate. All <u>members</u> of the family sat down to eat.

Spelling Regular Plurals, page 117

1. lives
2. attorneys
3. families
4. shelves
5. Churches
6. tomatoes
7. beliefs
8. companies

Spelling Irregular Plurals, page 118

1. scissors
2. fish
3. mice
4. teeth
5. glasses
6. feet
7. clothes
8. pants
9. people
10. women

Forming Singular Possessives, page 119

PART A

1. author's
2. Tan's
3. mother's
4. Pallas's
5. daughter's
6. novel's

PART B

1. the novel's plot
2. the reader's interest
3. the book's cover
4. the student's ideas

Forming Plural Possessives, page 120

PART A

1. tenants'
2. Golds'
3. families'
4. Schwartzes'
5. windows'
6. Smiths'
7. bedrooms'
8. landlords'

PART B

1. the attorneys' cases
2. several companies' products
3. the clients' complaints

Forming Irregular Possessives, page 121

PART A

1. the fishermen's boats
2. the children's toys
3. the women's uniforms
4. those mice's tails
5. the people's choice

PART B

The library's collection of books and magazines is impressive. The friendly staff works hard to meet people's needs. The children's room has books, magazines, CDs, DVDs, and computers. The room has won many parents' praise.

Chapter 8 Review—Nouns, page 122

1. Chicago
2. fire
3. buildings
4. ceremonies
5. men
6. May
7. tracks
8. Lake
9. Displays
10. street
11. movies
12. Jacks
13. Ferris
14. people
15. Ferris's
16. Sundays
17. United

Chapter 9: Pronouns

Identifying Pronouns, page 123

1. They
2. They, our
3. it
4. themselves
5. her
6. She, her
7. his
8. You, *I*, you, they
9. My, her

Using Subject Pronouns, page 124

PART A

1. He
2. It
3. He
4. She
5. They
6. We
7. you
8. it

PART B

Sentences will vary. Use these sentences as guidelines.

1. I would like to write a story.
2. She can help me think of a plot.
3. They will like my story.
4. It will be about a mysterious castle.

Using Object Pronouns I, page 125

PART A

1. him
2. us
3. them
4. it
5. us

6. her
7. her
8. them
9. you
10. it

PART B

Sentences will vary. Use these sentences as guidelines.

1. Please give him your attention.
2. We hired her to fill in the manager's position.
3. They gave us a refund.

Using Object Pronouns II, page 126

PART A

1. her
2. him
3. it
4. them
5. us
6. you
7. it
8. it

PART B

He asked <u>me</u> to read my essay aloud. He also asked Yolanda to read her essay to <u>him</u>. Then he gave <u>her</u> helpful advice.

Using Pronouns in Compounds, page 127

PART A

1. I
2. She
3. me
4. him
5. us
6. We, they
7. them

PART B

Neither their children nor <u>they</u> know how to cook it. The children sometimes take <u>him</u> and her out to eat. You and <u>I</u> should go with them sometime.

Using Possessive Pronouns I, page 128

PART A

1. their
2. They're
3. It's
4. its
5. your
6. You're

PART B

Sentences will vary. Use these sentences as a guideline.

1. Your job sounds very interesting.
2. His name is Hector.
3. The company changed its policy
4. Their children are a joy to be with.

Using Possessive Pronouns II, page 129

PART A

1. Mine
2. yours
3. Hers
4. Theirs
5. ours

PART B

1. theirs
2. mine
3. his
4. yours

Using Reflexive Pronouns, page 130

1. myself
2. himself
3. themselves
4. them
5. me
6. itself
7. I
8. you
9. yourselves
10. herself

Using Demonstrative Pronouns, page 131

PART A

1. that
2. Those
3. that

4. These
5. This

PART B

Sentences will vary. Use these sentences as guidelines.

1. Please bring me that file.
2. These cookies are delicious.
3. We enjoyed those cookies that you brought last week.

Chapter 9 Review–Pronouns, page 132

1. It's
2. This
3. its
4. they
5. their
6. them
7. they
8. I
9. themselves
10. These
11. them
12. us
13. This
14. her
15. himself
16. his
17. I
18. you

Chapter 10: Verbs

Identifying Verbs, page 133

1. is
2. had enlisted
3. worked
4. were formed
5. know
6. have served
7. banned
8. changed
9. can hold
10. are serving
11. are

Understanding Agreement, page 134

1. meet
2. serves
3. drive
4. live
5. know
6. quizzes
7. catches
8. confuse
9. helps
10. learn

Understanding Subject Nouns, page 135

1. He, plays
2. He, wins
3. He, hits
4. They, watch
5. She, sees
6. He, gives
7. It, supports
8. They, admire
9. He, sets
10. They, call
11. He, tries
12. We, love

Using Be, Have, and Do, page 136

1. is
2. has
3. has
4. are
5. do
6. are
7. is
8. have
9. has
10. do

Looking at Questions and Compounds, page 137

1. Do
2. forget
3. is
4. are
5. do
6. are
7. changes
8. Do
9. uses
10. Are
11. Have
12. is

Forming the Past Tense: Regular Verbs, page 138

1. decided
2. learned
3. married
4. washed
5. started
6. renamed
7. mixed
8. straightened
9. changed

Forming the Past Tense: Irregular Verbs, page 139

Folklorists from Indiana University ran the project. The folklorists were interested in old customs. Many people went to Gary, Indiana. They spoke about the cultures of their families. The folklorists saw how families followed traditions. Mrs. Meléndez told the group traditional folk tales. She said her family ate only Puerto Rican foods for many years. Philip wrote down what she said. I was glad that I attended.

Forming the Future Tense, page 140

PART A

1. will stop
2. will join
3. will be
4. will meet
5. will do
6. will return

PART B

Sentences will vary. Use these sentences as guidelines.

1. A week from now my candidate will win the election.
2. Next year my son will learn to drive.
3. Tomorrow Rita will make dinner.

Forming the Continuous Tenses, page 141

PART A

1. were
2. was
3. are
4. am
5. Are
6. is

PART B

Answers will vary. Use these sentences as guidelines.

1. I am writing a letter.
2. I was sleeping.
3. I will be washing the dishes.

Chapter 10 Review–Verbs, page 142

1. were
2. Are
3. were
4. lack
5. was
6. danced
7. made
8. delighted
9. faded
10. are
11. were
12. watch
13. rented
14. seen
15. go
16. show
17. Do
18. has
19. watch

Chapter 11: More About Verbs

Using the Present Perfect Tense, page 143

1. looked
2. has looked
3. have noticed
4. have complained
5. offered
6. refused

Using the Past Perfect Tense, page 144

1. was
2. had played
3. won
4. started
5. discovered
6. honored

7. have received
8. clapped
9. have learned

Using Irregular Verbs I, page 145

1. are, were, been
2. become, became, become
3. break, broken, broke
4. blows, blew, blown
5. brings, brought, brought

Using Irregular Verbs II, page 146

1. come, came, come
2. does, did, done
3. drinks, drank, drunk
4. eats, ate, eaten
5. freezes, frozen, froze

Using Irregular Verbs III, page 147

1. go, gone, went
2. grows, grown, grew
3. has, had, had
4. runs, run, ran
5. see, saw, seen

Using Irregular Verbs IV, page 148

1. speaks, spoken, spoke
2. steal, stole, stolen
3. take, took, taken
4. tells, told, told
5. writes, written, wrote

Forming the Passive Voice, page 149

1. faced
2. seen
3. rushed
4. kidnapped
5. paid
6. carried
7. asked
8. followed
9. robbed
10. shown

Using Participles, page 150

PART A

1. frozen
2. remodeled
3. revised
4. baked
5. closed
6. peeled
7. ironed

PART B

1. fallen
2. Covered
3. frozen
4. stored
5. increased

Using Fixed-Form Helpers, page 151

PART A

1. could use
2. must have
3. may attend
4. should take
5. can learn
6. might try
7. will start
8. will go

PART B

Sentences will vary. Use these sentences as a guideline.

1. Since I received my license, I can drive.
2. May I go with you?
3. We should practice driving every day.
4. I must drive under the speed limit.

Chapter 11 Review–More About Verbs, page 152

1. can look
2. have printed
3. might describe
4. known
5. was written
6. was limited
7. created
8. had defined
9. revised
10. have become
11. misspelled
12. had been
13. is done

Chapter 12: Adjectives and Adverbs

Identifying Adjectives, page 153

1. this
2. Few
3. remote
4. main
5. seven
6. clay
7. huge
8. smaller
9. good
10. shorter
11. roof
12. storage
13. Korean
14. ancient
15. These

Finding Adjectives in Sentences, page 154

1. A, sensible
2. B, innocent
3. A, weird
4. B, strange
5. B, reasonable
6. B, one
7. A, illegal
8. A, funny
9. B, mountain
10. B, another
11. B, Debt
12. B, police
13. B, My
14. B, unusual

Identifying Adverbs, page 155

PART A

1. c
2. a
3. b

PART B

1. there
2. often
3. very
4. quickly
5. well

Forming Adjectives and Adverbs, page 156

1. secretly, secret
2. complete, completely
3. perfect, perfectly
4. frequently, frequent
5. successfully, successful

Choosing Adjectives or Adverbs, page 157

PART A

1. loud
2. completely
3. hopeful
4. patiently
5. slowly
6. clearly
7. unusual
8. active
9. truly
10. famous

PART B

Actually his singing is awful. We all leave the room quickly when he singd. If he sang quietly, it wouldn't be so bad. But his voice is loud enough to hear in the next room!

Making Comparisons with Adjectives, page 158

1. tougher
2. least modest
3. most famous
4. strongest
5. faster
6. less skilled

Using Irregular Adjectives, page 159

PART A

1. best
2. better
3. worst
4. worse

PART B

I think it is better than any other detective show. The worst TV show is *Fear Factor*. I think it is worse than *Survivor*.

Making Comparisons with Adverbs, page 160

1. harder
2. less rapidly
3. more fully
4. less often
5. better
6. most actively
7. more frequently
8. best
9. well

Revising Double Negatives, page 161

1. a
2. a
3. b
4. b
5. b
6. a
7. b

Chapter 12 Review–Adjectives and Adverbs, page 162

1. whirling
2. most
3. worst
4. unbelievably
5. any
6. least
7. Entire
8. almost
9. more
10. Large
11. better
12. poorly
13. best
14. tirelessly
15. impressive
16. less
17. slowly
18. aren't

Chapter 13: Sentence Structure

Using End Marks, page 163

1. !
2. .
3. . (or !)
4. ?
5. .
6. .
7. ?

Understanding Simple Sentences, page 164

1. Most slave owners / didn't want . . .
2. Mrs. Auld / broke . . .
3. This slave owner / taught . . .
4. Mr. Auld / beat . . .
5. Douglass / escaped . . .
6. He / began . . .
7. People / were inspired . . .
8. Douglass / wrote . . .
9. The book / is called . . .
10. You / should read . . .
11. Douglass / held . . .
12. He / served . . .

Understanding Compound Sentences I, page 165

1. and
2. , so
3. , for
4. , but
5. or
6. , yet

Understanding Compound Sentences II, page 166

1. ; furthermore, (*Also correct are* moreover *and* in addition.)
2. ; however, (*Also correct is* on the other hand.)
3. ; as a result, (*Also correct are* therefore *and* thus.)
4. ; in addition, (*Also correct are* moreover *and* furthermore.)
5. ; therefore, (*Also correct are* as a result *and* thus.)
6. ; otherwise,

Fixing Run-Ons and Comma Splices, page 167

Corrections will vary. Use these corrections as a guideline.

The computer worked just fine at first; however, one day the computer would not start. Richardo thought someone at a nearby repair shop could help him, so he took the computer to the shop. The clerk said the computer was old; as a result, they could not fix it. Richardo was disappointed, but he was not going to give up. The computer wasn't very old. Why couldn't it be repaired?

The yellow pages had a list of computer repair shops. Other shops were advertised in the newspaper. Richardo called two shops, and his son called several others. The man at one shop said he could help; therefore, Richardo took the computer in. The repair took only a few minutes. A battery needed to be replaced. Richardo's computer worked well when he took it home; moreover, the repair had cost only $20.

Understanding Complex Sentences I, page 168

1. while she was growing up
2. After Margaret married J. J. Brown,
3. because they wanted a bigger house
4. so she could return from her vacation
5. Until the ship started sinking,
6. if she could get to a lifeboat
7. Although Margaret was tired from rowing,
8. since she survived her trip on the *Titanic*

Understanding Complex Sentences II, page 169

1. that some adults believe in
2. , which are not supported with evidence,
3. who believe in Bigfoot
4. , who worked for the Smithsonian Institution,
5. , which is similar to Bigfoot.

Correcting Sentence Fragments I, page 170

Corrections will vary. Use these corrections as a guideline.

The problem is the increasing cost of insurance premiums, which are too expensive for many people. Millions of people are suffering because they need medical care but do not have insurance. Every day there are children who do not get medical care. Although many families have medical insurance, they may not be able to afford it in the future. This problem has been recognized by political leaders such as Ted Kennedy, Hillary Clinton, and Barack Obama, who are all members of the U.S. Senate.

Correcting Sentence Fragments II, page 171

Corrections will vary. Use these corrections as a guideline.

Many people tried to help whenever there was a fire in the city. But they did not have equipment or know how to fight fires. In 1735 Franklin sent a letter to his own newspaper. He suggested that the same group of men always travel with a fire engine. By practicing, they would learn how to fight fires. They could also hold meetings to discuss fire prevention. Franklin's ideas were the beginning of modern fire departments.

Chapter 13 Review–Sentence Structure, page 172

1. a
2. b
3. a
4. a
5. b
6. b
7. a
8. b
9. a